beautiful
behaviors

Chris Schimel

CREATION
HOUSE
A STRANG COMPANY

BEAUTIFUL BEHAVIORS by Chris Schimel
Published by Creation House
A Strang Company
600 Rinehart Road
Lake Mary, Florida 32746
www.creationhouse.com

Author's note: some names have been changed to protect identities.

English definitions are derived from *Funk & Wagnalls Standard Desk Dictionary*, vol. 1. New York: Harper & Row Publishers, 1964.

Greek definitions are derived from *Treasures of the Greek New Testament*, Kenneth S. Wuest. Grand Rapids, MI: Wm. B. Eerdmans Publishing Co., 1941.

Cover design by Terry Clifton

Library of Congress Control Number: 2007931874
International Standard Book Number: 978-1-59979-247-7

First Edition

07 08 09 10 11 — 9 8 7 6 5 4 3 2 1
Printed in the United States of America

☙ Contents ❧

❧ *Introduction* ❧

BEFORE I BEGIN, it is important that I clarify: the behaviors of beauty I address in this book may be found in an individual church, or they may not. They might be found in an individual—hopefully you. Most definitely they refer to and can be found in members of the Church of Jesus Christ.

If you are the leader of a group of people and you desire to see these traits become formed in your church or fellowship, you seek a noble objective—albeit a lofty one. However, if you can begin to see reflections of these "beautiful behaviors" lived out in your life and the lives of some of the people in your group, I can't imagine people not being attracted to the group you lead just because they crave the beauty they see.

In the nearly forty years I have been in the ministry, I have seen much beauty, as well as much ugliness, in the church. I love and prefer the beauty; I detest and resist the ugly.

The beauty of the church has nothing to do with a worship band, a youth ministry, a set of values, or even church growth. The beauty of the church has precious little to do with the outward appearance of a property, the value of a building, the order in a set of financial books, or the charisma or reputation of a church leader. It doesn't have to do with the performance of a liturgy or how the members dress or adorn themselves. It doesn't have to do with how relevant or sensitive a church is to its culture or how big or small a group of believers may be.

The beauty of the church—the Bride of Christ—has to do with how people, groups, and individuals, reflect the glory and character of the Bridegroom. Do they truly look like Christ? Do they cause people to stop and say, "My, isn't she beautiful! But isn't Jesus glorious!"

Hebrews 1:3 refers to the "brightness of *His* glory" (emphasis added). The beauty of the bride will always give way to the glory of the groom.

As a minister I have performed many weddings. The most beautiful are so not because of the setting, the colors, the attire, the decorations, or the perfection of the ceremony.

I once performed a wedding in a legendary marriage spot in California. Both families of the bride and groom were quite wealthy; consequently, money wasn't an object, so no expenses were spared. Elements included a pricy wedding coordinator, escorts, limousines, and guests flying in from all over the world at the two families' expenses—and more. The view was breathtaking. The colors were gorgeous. The guests and wedding party were proper and flawless in their dress and performance. The buildings around the site were perfectly designed for wedding events and pristinely maintained. It was picturesque—a sight to behold.

But something was missing. I couldn't put my finger on it until I saw this missing element—present in a wedding I performed sometime after that one. It was the awe of the bride for her groom. This awe encompassed love, respect, honor, and cherishing.

Some brides are too preoccupied with the details of the wedding to be free to demonstrate their deepest feelings for their husbands-to-be. Some are grieved by mistakes people have made in the preparations. Some are exhausted. Some are embarrassed by a song sung or a number played off-key. I recall one bride who appeared to be on the verge of utter despair as she stood in front of me listening to the out-of-tune performance of the soloist she had been pressured to let sing.

But when the bride is in awe of her groom, and the groom in deepest love with his bride—when no details of the ceremony, courtship, or pre-wedding rituals are influential enough to distract them from each other; when love, respect, passion, and honor are observed in their hearts between each other—everything is more beautiful, more touching, more meaningful, more joyous. It is so because the relationship and character of the people involved has brought substance to the future marriage and renewed hope to the whole idea of matrimony. That is what makes a bride beautiful, a groom handsome, and the event itself the celebration it is intended to be. It is a beautiful thing.

True beauty is seen in a wedding when mutual and obvious love is apparent between the bride and the groom, and no details or concerns are able to distract them from each other. "Impossible," you say? Not so, I've seen it happen.

Now let's bring the analogy back to the church of Jesus Christ. The bride (or the church) is most beautiful when she sheds light on the glory of the groom—who is Christ. The integrity of the relationship between the two is believable and on display for all to see.

In *Beautiful Behaviors* we talk about the actions of those who belong to the church of Jesus Christ. We talk about individual groups or expressions of the church that are so beautiful; yet rather than bring attention to their own beauty, they point directly to the glory of Christ. And they bring credence to the belief in God's existence, His love for the world and His people, and the genuineness of the church's relationship with its God.

You may notice as you read that the growth of any group is not my intention in writing this book. This is not a church growth book. It is a church beautification book. Its purpose is to develop beauty in the members and the gatherings of Christ's body, that all of us might become the beautiful bride Jesus desires us to be. I also desire that the true beauty of Christ's church become exposed for all to see.

Part I

∞ *The Beauty of Liberty* ∞

"IVE ME LIBERTY or give me death" was the cry of the early American patriot Patrick Henry. But I am not so sure it is *not* also the cry of many people in our world where relationship with God, Christians, and churches are concerned.

I run into people with regularity who cite as their reason for scarcity in their church attendance, "There are too many rules." And I am not only talking about blatant heathens. I am also talking about professed Christians. I connect with believers often who feel so alienated and judged by the people and standards of churches they used to attend that the joy of their relationship with the Lord simply left, and not long after they departed from the church they had attended for many years. My heart breaks for them because I know it doesn't need to be so. A church and Christians can adhere to every sound standard in the Holy Book's pages and still not cause people to feel judged or alienated by those standards.

In this section we talk about six behaviors that I believe will bring a sense of overwhelming freedom to your church as well as to the hearts of individuals who attend.

Chapter 1

❧

Leverage-Free Environment

O NE OF THE most powerful forces known to man is: Grandma. Who can say "no" to a feeble old woman with a job she needs to have done? The word feeble, of course, is just *dressing*. The whole family knows Grandma is anything but feeble. She's a force. She's a giant. She's a power. And she knows it, and they know it. She wields the power with expert and careful precision. And they fall powerless before her time and time again.

Consider the errand Grandma needs to have run. She mentions it at dinner with the whole family present. It must be run now. It can't wait for tomorrow, the weekend, or next week because Grandma wants (no, needs) it done now.

When no one can take the time to perform the task, Grandma says, "Oh...OK then. I guess I'll have to do it myself. Don't worry about it. I'll take care of it."

Of course everyone can see the disappointment in Grandma's eyes. It isn't obvious. She hides it well enough so that no one can say with a certainty that she let it be seen with the intent to manipulate. But deep down, they all know.

Finally a nephew and a son-in-law speak up at the same time. "I suppose I could run up there this afternoon," they both say almost in unison.

There's a small skirmish as to who will actually run the errand, nephew or son-in-law. One wins (or loses, depending on your perspective. And the power play is over. Grandma is the real winner.

Over and over this saga is played out within families to which many of us belong.

But leverage doesn't stop with Grandma. Oh no. It trickles into families at every level. Wives manipulate husbands. Parents manipulate kids. Kids wield it over their moms and dads, and brothers and sisters do the same over each other. This is learned and passed down to subsequent generations. But even family systems aren't the end of leverage.

Consider schools, their activities, and their influence.

When I was in school, educational budgets were very different than they are today. I could play basketball, baseball, and football and participate in dramas, plays, and other activities with no charges to me or my family. Uniform costs, equipment expenses, and trips to games and events were all free.

Nowadays things have changed dramatically. If your son or daughter wants to play sports or participate in another school activity, it could cost you an arm and a leg.

I have a brother-in-law who has two very athletic girls in grade school. They are skilled in gymnastics, so they joined the cheerleading/dance team. Though it cost some money for uniforms and other entrance fees, Mom and Dad thought it was a good investment. After all, it was wholesome for their girls. It contributed to a healthy self-esteem for their daughters. And it gave them opportunities to build healthy relationships with young girls their own age.

Several weeks into the season Mom and Dad learned of a cheerleading competition the team had a chance to enter in Florida. And it was only going to cost $4,000.

Consider with me the leverage that began to be applied to my brother-in-law.

First the "L" word came from his two pleading daughters.

"Please…Daddy…pleeeease! Everyone on the team is going. If we don't go, we will be the only ones not there. And they need us because we are the point leaders for several of the cheers. The whole team will lose if we aren't there."

Then there were the coaches.

"If there is any way you can send your daughters, it would be great for the team. It will be an excellent experience for your girls, and frankly we don't think the team has a chance to win without your daughters being there."

Then consider the town.

The village they live in is quite small. Just imagine the fallout from the whole town if he doesn't let his girls go and the team loses because they aren't there—especially since he has been advised by the coaches concerning how important his daughters are to the team's success. You can just picture the angry stares and the people talking behind their backs. And yes, he would even chance his girls being treated poorly and not given consideration on future teams and activities they may want to take part in. "Silly," you say? If you think so, you've never lived in a small town.

Then, there is the girl's Mom to my brother-in-law.

"You go skiing pretty much any time you want and that is no inexpensive endeavor. Now here is a chance for your daughters to have an experience of a lifetime. How can you say no to them?"

Friends, that's leverage!

But the "L" word doesn't stop there. Oh, no. Have you ever paused to consider the leverage being imposed on the consuming public by the marketplace powers of our world?

The ads aren't this honest, but they are this accurate:

- Buy this car so you can showcase to your friends, relatives, neighbors, and acquaintances how successful you have become.

- Purchase our safe, well-made, and expensive automobile so your family will know that you truly love them. Buy what you can afford and they will wonder.

- Acquire your clothes from our "what's happening now" line of name-brand apparel so your friends will know you are the coolest. If you don't, you chance friendlessness.

- Buy our house. You won't be able to say you have achieved the American dream unless you own one of our "state of the art" homes on one of our picturesque properties. You want to be the superior one among your relatives—don't you?

- Buy our fitness equipment so you can have the slim trim body you see on the models in our ads—even though we all know that the chance you will ever look like them is equivalent your chance of being struck by lightening.

- Take a trip to our vacation spot so you can impress your friends, save your family, and preserve your soon-to-be lost-from-stress life.

It's all leverage—nothing pure, nothing honest, nothing of concern for you.

- Our fast-food restaurant cares.

- Our law firm truly cares.

- Our car rental company genuinely cares.

- Our doctors and dentists honestly care.

- Our HMO is the only one that really cares.

- Our nationally known department store cares— cares—cares.

It's all leverage. More than 99 percent of all consumer products care only about one thing: getting as much of your money into their pockets as they can. They use marketing leverage devices and tricks to lure you into their establishments so they can pocket more of your money.

In fact, let's be gut-level honest. If you listened to their ads and spent every dime of your money at their store, and as a result lost your home and ended up on the streets feeding yourself from trashcans, they wouldn't care one lick. They would continue to use their sales tactics—laden with leverage—in an attempt to garner as much of the next guys' money as they possibly can.

And it is effective. All this leverage is designed to get you to buy—buy—buy. And it works—works—works.

Leverage—leverage—leverage. It is imposed upon us from every level of our society and culture.

Let's be even more honest.

Many Christians and churches are no different.

In my early ministry years, I used a short illustration at the end of some of my sermons in order to persuade people to become Christians. It went something like this.

"If you walked out the back doors of the church after this service is over and were killed in a car accident, would you be ready to go to heaven? Could you honestly say you know you would end up in paradise if that happened? If you can't say for sure, then you need to come to the front of the church and give your heart to the Lord right now."

It was an arm-twisting method because every non-Christian in the world and many Christians could not say for sure that they would end up in heaven if they died today. The Bible does infer that we can know, but most Christians have to come to a place where biblical knowledge and spiritual assurance have increased commensurate with their maturity in Christ in order to have this confidence. The issue of people becoming Christians has much more to do with their desire to surrender their lives to Christ than whether or not they are sure they would go to heaven if they were to die right then. I was leveraging the people by manipulating the fear and ignorance that I suspected was existent in their hearts.

Not that many people responded. I guess they were too smart to be manipulated by such a ploy. I think, though, that deep inside my heart I knew it was manipulative. But I justified it by saying, "It is for a good cause. I really want to see people come to Christ. So if I insert a little leverage into the mix, it's OK because my intentions are good." It is just a tiny example of how Christians can use leverage in their ministry methods.

But it can get worse—much worse. Christians, churches, and church leaders are notorious for using leverage to accomplish their goals.

They exert leverage with money and giving because more money means more accomplishments.

They employ leverage with church attendance and numbers because larger crowds feed their egos.

They use leverage to get people to perform tasks and functions because people can be a means to the ends of their success.

But in any setting, church or otherwise, leverage can create anger, resentment, and long-term bitterness in the hearts of those being leveraged.

Think with me about the leverage people have to deal with every day. Many have to endure it in their families (starting with Grandma) and with their relatives in the form of dysfunctional family systems. They have to endure it with their neighbors who maneuver it into their backyard, over-the-fence relationships. They have to endure it at work where they find themselves jockeying for position in relationships, promotions, raises, and just finding ways to survive. They have to deal with it in their kid's school relationships and the P.T.A. They have to deal with leverage from the media and television shows and commercials. And who can count the many other ways we are leveraged in our world today? By the time they get to the church they are all leveraged out—they're exhausted.

People shouldn't have to confront a Christian or come to a church and be made to feel guilty, condemned, manipulated, and leveraged—at least not by humans trying to play the role of the Holy Spirit. People should be able to connect with a true Christian or come to church and feel freedom, peace, hope, and loved by God and man.

The irony in it all is this: God's word gives instructions on how to drape ministry gatherings and our redemptive relationships with people in a "leverage-free environment."

Jesus tells us in John 8:36, "Whom I set free shall be free indeed" (my paraphrase). What does "free indeed" really mean? Without philosophizing too much, let's just say it means "really free." Let's talk about being "really free."

We live in a world that is profoundly confused about the concept of freedom. The reason: No one has a crosshair's bead on the true meaning of freedom.

I'll tell you what freedom is not. It is not the absence of restraint. It is not financial freedom. It is not living without bars or chains. It is not even having Jesus in our hearts, because I have seen plenty of Christians with Jesus living in their hearts who are all bound up with rules, legalism, power plays, and leverage.

When I was a kid growing up in church, it seemed everything was a sin. At least that is what the church leaders told us, and our parents took on the task of reinforcing it. Going to movies was a sin. Dancing was a sin. Roller skating was a sin. Ice skating was a sin. Drinking alcohol was a sin. Short skirts were a sin. Tattoos were a sin. Earrings were a sin, to say nothing of nose rings, eyebrow rings, tongue rings, and belly button rings. Computers were a sin. Cheerleading was a sin. Holding hands was a sin. Tight pants were a sin. Now baggy pants are a sin. Wearing shorts was a sin. Two-piece bathing suits were a sin. Running in church was a sin. Smoking was a sin. Listening to rock music was a sin. Talking about rock music was a sin. Thinking about rock music was a sin. And that was the short list.

If you were ever caught doing or saying any of these things, you could almost feel the fires of hell closing in on you.

By the time I had been through Bible college and in the ministry for four years, I had shed a great deal of the guilt I felt about most of those things, and one was going to movies. But the church I was working for as youth pastor was not as liberated as I was. They weren't at all in favor of their staff personnel attending movies; not so much because they felt it was wrong, but because some church members still felt it was a sin. The church leadership didn't want the staff to offend the church members by going to movies. I had just accepted a position in California and submitted my resignation. Friends asked me if my wife and I wanted to go with them to a movie. It was Christmas time and the new movie *King Kong*, a remake of the original version, was playing. We figured we would be gone from that church in a week, so why not? We said yes, but I struggled with that decision. Though I would be leaving in less than a week, I knew how the pastors of the church felt about it. What if they found out?

When we arrived at the theatre, we stepped into line to buy tickets. From that point on I was a nervous wreck. I glanced about fretfully to see if someone else would be at the theatre who might report my indiscretion to my current superiors. My panic had me thinking irrationally that I would be found out and reported, and that would be the end of my ministry. I couldn't wait to get my ticket and slip into the theatre where I could slither down in my seat and hide in the dark. While the movie was playing, my stress level subsided as I became caught up in the story—but not entirely. As the picture concluded and we began to exit the theatre, I felt my anxiety level rise again.

And sure enough, as we were leaving, my keen and nervous eyes caught a glimpse of a family from the church. Before I could hide behind another exit door, they spotted us and waved.

I knew my ministry was over. They would report it to the pastor. The pastor would call my new overseer and that would be it. My sins would find me out.

That is the kind of fear and bondage my early church experience formed in my heart.

Today it is no different. The issues have changed, but man still tries to place religious burdens on people.

I don't understand how we as Christians can become so bound up with rules and regulations considering the Bible's descriptions about liberty and the freedom we have in Christ. But we do.

Let's look at Paul's explanation of Christian liberty.

In 1 Corinthians chapters 6 and 10, four times Paul makes this statement, "All things are lawful for me" (1 Cor. 6:12; 10:23).

When Paul said this, what did he mean? This may blow some people away, but he means he can do anything and still be a Christian. Why can Paul say this? He can say it because he had a vice-grip on understanding the power of Christ's blood to save and cleanse us from sin. He knew that his position in Christ and the power of Christ's blood gave him unlimited liberty to do whatever he wanted.

Now before anyone jumps to any outrageous conclusions about my walk with God and my understanding of scripture, let me quote the next part of Paul's verses. He said, "All things are lawful...but not all things are helpful." That means, as a Christian I am free to do all things, but all things are not necessarily beneficial or good for me.

If I am a Christian, can I smoke and go to heaven? Can I miss church on Sundays and still walk arm and arm with Saint Peter? Can I go to an R-rated movie and still get through those pearly gates? Can I go dancing and listen to gangster rap and still walk on streets of gold? Yes, yes, yes, and yes. But some of these may affect my physical health, kill me prematurely, make my walk with God less effective, or create guilt feelings between me and my Savior that could cause me to live a defeated life in Christ.

In 1 Corinthians 6:12 Paul adds this thought, "All things are lawful for me, but I will not be brought under the power of any." This idea introduces another thought which suggests that some of these things we do that are lawful but not helpful can actually become points of bondage and can have a kind of power over us that may rob us of freedom and liberty in other ways.

Take gambling for example. The Bible doesn't address the subject directly, but Gamblers Anonymous will tell you the habit can have the same kind of effect on people as other addictive practices and substances. What can happen is a person can be controlled by it.

In my first church, a man won $4,000 one time at the slots. His eye to "get rich quick" (see Proverbs 28:22) took control of his life and he gambled the house away—twice—as well as the family nest egg. He had come under the power of the thing he chose to do.

In Christ we are free to do anything. But as God deals with our hearts about the expediency of those things, we are free and are often wise to say "no."

Before I was a Christian, I sowed some wild oats which included some drinking. Within a few years after I became a Christian, I developed a personal conviction that drinking wasn't for me. My thinking included three reasons. 1) It was a link to my past that I sensed God wanted me to leave behind. 2) One sip of beer, even as low in alcohol content as it was, made me feel light headed. This caused me to feel out of control—and this I didn't like. 3) I didn't like the taste of any kind of alcohol. So I decided early on in my walk with Christ that even social or light drinking wasn't for me. It may have been for others, but not for me.

One year when I came to my hometown for a vacation, I learned one of my old drinking buddies had bought a home and lived in a rural area nearby. So I went to visit him, and he was quite shocked to see me. He had heard I became a minister (everyone had), but within a few minutes he offered me a beer. When I said no he responded, "Come on, Chris. No one's here. No one will see you, and I'm not going to tell anyone. You can have one beer."

Granted, he probably had no idea about the power of change that comes to bear in a person that takes on Christ and therefore was clueless about the transformation that had taken place in my life. But he clearly assumed my relationship with God and the actions I was taking were being dictated to me by *men*, and I was living under the bondage of religious rules and not my own convictions. But that wasn't it at all. I was free to have a beer or smoke a cigarette or do anything else. But I was also free to not do any of those things. When I said "no," I was exercising my freedom.

Many people assume Christianity is confining. They feel it is a series of rules and regulations that are bent on placing anyone who signs on into bondage; that Christians can't do anything—say anything—or go anywhere. And I'll tell you where they get the idea. They get it from Christians who don't understand Christian liberty.

Do you remember when I said I had a struggle with going to the movies? Much of it was imposed on me from bad teaching concerning Christian liberty. I grew beyond that and to this day feel no condemnation at all about movie-going. The biggest problem I have with movies nowadays has to do with the price. I'm a little cheap. However, I did make a personal decision to not drink alcohol. That was my independent choice. I impose it on no one. I have Christian friends who consume a casual drink now and then, but I make no judgments about them and they make none about me.

The greatest influencer of people thinking that Christianity is laden with religious rules and regulations comes from Christians who impose their personal convictions—often personal bondages—onto other people. They roll their eyes when they see others do what they feel is wrong. They may sigh, turn away, act superior, or even scold others for their unrighteousness. Many Christians will do this. Church leaders will do this. Often entire church congregations will slip into this way of thinking and acting toward anyone they see. Churches and church members alike will poke, prod, persuade, squeeze, arm twist, roll their eyes, turn their heads in disgust, and use all manner of body language and manipulations of the scriptures in an effort to get people to do Christianity their way.

The result of this behavior is this: believers and non-believers have been reinforced in their prognosis about Christianity—it is a confining, rule-oriented, bondage-producing cramp to their lifestyle. Thus, many people feel the opposite is true of Jesus' words, "He whom Jesus sets free…is in serious bondage" (my paraphrase).

But any Christian with an ounce of biblical knowledge and perception can see this reeks of pharisaical trappings. It looks much like the scribes and religious leaders of Jesus' day. One would almost expect to see a group of first-century robed Pharisees, led by Caiaphas himself, walk off the pages of scripture and into the church that manipulates and leverages people in this manner. And when they burst on the scene, you can almost sense the approval they would give to the rule-infested, regulatory oppression that the church is imposing upon its members and any sinners that might happen through the doors.

That is why: beautiful is the Christian and attractive is the church environment that reflects more and more the liberty there is in Christ.

It is not a matter of condoning sin "that grace may abound" (Rom. 6:1). It is not a matter of ignoring sin. Nor is it loving the things of the world more than the things of God. And it isn't lowering our standards. It is a matter of having a strangle-hold grip on the scriptures' approach to Christian liberty as seen in Paul's theology and our Lord's example of loving, accepting, and forgiving people.

What kind of beauty would we behold if we could duplicate in our hearts and churches the kind of accepting, freeing, and leverage-absent environment that sinners and saints alike felt when they were around Jesus? Wow! I don't think we could keep people away.

The reality is this: in Christ there is no bondage at all, save the light yoke of obedience that Jesus talks about in Matthew 11:28–30 that actually brings rest and peace to its doers. That is why whom the Son sets free, is "really free," and where there is Christ, there is only liberty.

How will you live this out in your life? How will you teach this to your church? How will you endeavor to see this lived out in your fellowship of believers or your relationships with other people?

In the next chapter we will take "leverage-free" to the next level.

Chapter 2

~

A Place of Grace

WE TEND TO treat people the way we would like to be treated. If we feel we deserve a break, we give people a break. If we feel we deserve stringency, we are stringent toward others.

But that is not the way Jesus treats us. When we came to Him, He overlooked everything we ever did. And based upon our reception of His sacrifice on the cross for us, He completely forgave us and accepted us just the way we were. We deserved stringency; He gave us the break of a lifetime.

In effect, we tend to act differently toward people than Jesus acted toward us. We want people to cuss less, lust less, and fuss less than we did when we became Christians. When we came to Christ, we received limitless grace from the Lord. Yet, as other people are trying to come to Him, and as Jesus is trying to offer them the same limitless grace He presented to us, we are trying to complicate people's approach of Jesus by imposing our learned Christian disciplines and maturities on them. It confuses people because they need grace, and they don't understand our post-salvation disciplines and maturities—at least not yet.

When I first became a Christian, I heard a definition of grace. I have never heard a better one. It is "unmerited favor," that is, "mercy extended that is not deserved."

In the first church we led as senior pastors, we began to see many people come to church who were unsaved. When they heard the gospel message, they responded to it enthusiastically. But as I watched, I found they didn't change their manner of living immediately. After becoming Christians, some would continue to do drugs, overindulge in alcohol, use foul language, live together outside of marriage, etc.

I had a choice. I could speak to them about their lifestyle, which I really wanted to do and which I did a few times. Or I could extend to them the same grace Jesus afforded me when I first came to Christ. I decided I would give the latter option a try and graciously, but truthfully, address the subjects from the pulpit. But I would love and accept them the way they were—sin, warts, blemishes, and all. I didn't deserve this treatment from the Lord when I came to Him, but received it nonetheless. I tried to treat them the way Jesus treated me. I found that they changed quickly, willingly, and permanently when I did this.

A revelation occurred to me. When I spoke to people about their sin directly, they knew I was right, and they tried to change with minimal results. But when I taught God's word in love and truth, treating them with grace and acceptance, it created an environment that enabled them to respond to the voice of God—a much more influential voice than mine. And when people heard the Holy Spirit's voice instead of my own, their life change was much more rapid, much more their desire, and much more enduring than if I had spoken to them.

If people came and asked me, I would tell them; and I was prepared to speak to them if their lifestyle became destructive to themselves or others in the church. But they never did. So I endeavored to let the Holy Spirit do the speaking.

The results were incredible. Looking back, I think I stumbled into a mindset that fostered an environment of grace—one that allowed people to flourish in their personal walks with God and one in which people felt safe.

For example, one situation involved a man named Rick. Rick came to the Lord and soon afterward started coming to our church. He worked for a large Fun Park with arcades, batting cages, and miniature golf. He was genuinely converted to Christ, and when he started attending our church, he brought his family with him. One day after he had been coming for several weeks, he called me.

He said, "Pastor, would you be able to come over to my house? I have something I need to show you."

I hopped into my car and drove the few blocks' distance to his house. As I pulled up to his home and parked in front, I could see he was outside waiting for me. When I got out of my car, he motioned for me to follow him over to his vehicle. He opened the rear hatch and pointed to a duffle bag that was sitting in among the miscellaneous equipment inside the trunk. I could see it was partially open and that it was nearly full of change.

He said, "See that? I always have plenty of money. I make a pretty good living, plus I have all the change I want from the money boxes in the machines." "But," he went on, "I haven't been able to touch that duffle bag since last week. I guess I always knew it was wrong for me to take it, but something you said in your sermon last Sunday got to me. I've been doing this for a couple of years, and now, all of a sudden, I can't touch it and I don't know what to do with it. What do you think I should do?"

I was a little taken aback and wasn't quite sure what to say. But I responded, "I don't know, Rick. What do you think you should do with it?"

He said, "Well, God won't let me spend it. I don't feel right about giving it to someone. And it doesn't make sense to throw it away. If I go to my bosses and tell them what I've been doing, they will fire me and throw me in jail. I have a house, a wife, a little girl, and one on the way. They won't do well with me in prison. My wife will likely divorce me if that happened. But that is probably what I am going to have to do."

Right then I was faced with a decision. I could think rules and regulations, or I could think grace.

I asked, "Rick, how easy is it for you to steal that change?"

Rick said, "It's easy. I could take three hundred dollars a day if I wanted." Then he looked at me a little funny and asked, "Why, do you want me to get some for you?"

"No," I chuckled. "I just figured if it was easy for you to take it out of the machines, it might also be easy for you to put it back in the machines."

A light came on in Rick's soul and manifested itself on his face. He thought I was going to say that he needed to go to his superiors with his head bowed and his hands out in front of him ready to receive the cuffs when they snapped them onto him. But when my response suggested that his life and walk with God may *not* require his destruction after all, he was elated.

Almost jumping up and down he said, "I can put it all back real easy. I can do it tomorrow. Thank you, pastor."

Some might criticize me for my advice. Regulatory people may think my solution a compromise.

But here was my thinking.

First, Rick was a changed man. I had no doubt that the Holy Spirit had spoken to him and had spoken loud and clear. What he was showing me and his accompanying attitude was a sign of someone who had experienced a divinely legitimate transformation in his life. Rick had met God. And as God was speaking, Rick was hearing.

Next, as he was presenting the scenario to me, my mind had been racing through the Bible knowledge I had by then and stopped on the story of the woman caught in adultery in the Gospel of John, chapter 8. I rapidly assessed the account and surmised—Rick deserved to be taken away, jailed, and suffer the consequence of losing his house and his family, just as the woman before Jesus deserved to be stoned for her sin.

But that is not what Jesus gave to the woman. He told her, "Neither do I condemn you; go and sin no more" (v. 11). And I thought, "How could I say to Rick the same kind of thing Jesus said to the woman?"

So, in effect, the words "Go put the money back and never do it again" sounded to me like Jesus' response to the woman. It sounded like God's grace, mercy, and affirmation for the transformation in Rick's life, as well as standing up for righteousness at the same time. I also figured if God wanted him to pay more severely for his crime, He could always arrange for an employee to catch him returning the money.

Rick put the money back and never took another penny. He became one of the most dynamic members and leaders in our church. He led his family into the faith and literally dozens of people to Christ. I am reasonably sure if I had thought rules and regulations that day instead of grace and mercy, things would have been very different for Rick, his family, and our church.

Would I have advised something similar if there had been a dead body in the trunk instead of a bag full of change? I should hope not. But looking back with hindsight, I am reasonably sure I would have tried to discover what might have been Jesus' most gracious response and suggested that.

Another incident of grace also occurred in our first church. Many people who weren't Christians began attending and seeking a relationship with the Lord. Soon I learned that many of these constituted couples (some with children, some without) who weren't married. In time, one by one, these couples came to the altar to receive Christ. And it was very exciting to see. At one point I counted nine couples in all.

As I observed them, however, I discovered they weren't submitting to the sacred vows of marriage as quickly as they were to the Lord's call to become Christians. And so again, I was faced with a decision. I could think rules and regulations, or I could think grace and mercy. Believe me, I was very tempted to set up individual meetings with these couples and straighten out their theology.

But something told me that strict approach was not the one I should take. Instead, I decided I would carefully address the subject out of God's Word from the pulpit and let God speak. I also decided that when I talked to them after church and at fellowships, I would treat them as if they were the most awesome Christians on the face of the earth. Now, I knew I was taking a chance doing this because it might communicate to them that I condoned their "live-in" relationship and they might continue to avoid marriage.

But it didn't have that effect at all. One by one, just as they had come to Christ, they came to me and told me that God was speaking to them about getting married, and would I be willing to marry them?

When they started to come, I was faced with still another decision. Should I simply marry them, or should I encourage them to make a statement of righteousness and live apart until the wedding? After all, they were Christians now; they should want to submit to that standard of morality. I had heard of pastors who had done that, and I admired the boldness and stand for purity of that approach. But I wasn't sure it was the approach I should take.

To seek advice, I went to a leader I deeply respected. Interestingly, I knew him to be a bit rigid, and I expected him to lean in the regulatory direction, but I trusted his wisdom.

This is what he told me.

"Why would you ask them to traumatize their whole living situation? If they have been living together for any length of time, it will be a major adjustment for them to change, even if just financially. They have already made a healthy and right decision to get married. Why would you punish them for doing the right thing? When Zacchaeus became a follower of Christ, Jesus didn't tell him to leave his friends or even to stop what he was doing. Instead, Jesus went to Zacchaeus' house and hung out with him and his sinner friends. While Jesus and his disciples were there, Zacchaeus was the one who stood and announced to Jesus in everyone's hearing about his conversion and told them about the change God had made in his life. Jesus never spoke a word to him about changing his lifestyle. At least there is no record of it in scripture. Jesus just accepted him the way he was. Their decisions to come to you to be married are an indication that God spoke to them already. They've already gotten the message. Why do you feel you need to make more of a statement to them than what God has already told them?"

Wow! I was blown away. What wisdom. What insight. What grace. Mostly it was a confirmation of my own reluctance to saddle them with a stipulation.

I began to perform weddings with joy in my heart that God was indeed solemnizing these marriages in His grace and mercy.

One of these couples was Eddie and Pat. They started coming to church, and within a few weeks they both gave their hearts to Christ. And their conversion was real. Both cried and repented of their sins and received Christ into their hearts as Lord. I expected that within a few more weeks they would come and ask me to marry them.

But they didn't.

A month went by, and still no call—then two months, then three, then four. They were in church every Sunday morning, every Sunday night, and every Wednesday night. They heard God's word each time they came, and you can be sure they were getting the message.

Six months, then seven went by and still no call from Eddie and Pat about getting married. I was very close to violating my code, when after eight months, I received a call from Eddie.

Eddie said, "Pastor Chris, Pat and I have been talking and we have decided to do something we should have done a while ago. I don't know if you know this or not, but Pat and I aren't married."

I said with surprise and wonder, "You're not?"

"No," said Eddie. "And we both feel God wants us to do that. Would you be willing to marry us? We have a date in mind."

What Eddie didn't know was that inside my heart I was doing flips. I was so happy. But I wasn't happy that finally this couple living outside of marriage was getting married. No. I was rejoicing in the power of God's voice to speak to His children about His will for them. And I was ecstatically silly that I had not gotten out in front of God's grace. I had relied on His grace and His voice to change this couple—and together they had.

Eddie and Pat became some of the most dynamic children's teachers and leaders I have ever seen in the ministry. They compiled a team of children's workers and literally transformed our Kids' Ministries. They are strong and growing believers and Christians to this day.

SPIRITUALLY DEAD

There are some things that must happen in order for grace to dominate your heart or the environment of your church.

Before a person becomes a Christian, that person is "dead in trespasses and sins" (Eph. 2:1). That means they have no spiritual life inside them. Neither do they have a propensity toward this spiritual life or an understanding of how it works. For me to expect a non-Christian to not lie, cuss, drink, fornicate, adulterate, do drugs, or hate the in-laws shows a complete ignorance of biblical instruction on the issue. They are dead to God—spiritually dead. If I treat them as if they should know better, I've missed the whole point of conversion and new life in Christ.

Jesus understood this fact of spiritual deadness very well. That is how He could hang with sinners, accept them just the way they were, and never speak a correcting word to them.

He knew that to scold a sinner for transgression was like scolding an infant for failing to put on his coat. An infant doesn't know why he needs a coat and wouldn't be able to put it on if he did. A sinner's spiritual deadness reacts the same way. We accept and love babies in their ignorance. Jesus did the same with sinners.

The Pharisees and religious leaders had no clue what spiritual deadness was, let alone how to apply it to their relationship with sinners. In fact, they were so confused by the concept, not only were they judgmental of the sinners Jesus was with, they also judged Jesus for being with them—suggesting He and the sinners both came out of the same mold.

Jesus told a parable in Matthew 20:1–15 about people's inability to understand God's grace. You can read the entire account yourself, but let me give you my brief paraphrased version for easy reference.

A landowner was looking for men to work in his vineyard. He visited the local labor pool at six and nine in the morning and picked out several guys who were eager to work. He told them he would pay them a fair day's wage when the day was done. They agreed and went to work for the man. Later he discovered he needed more workers to get the job done, so at noon and three in the afternoon he went by the labor pool and found some other men who needed work. He agreed to pay them fairly, so they signed on with him. At five in the afternoon, the vineyard owner was wandering through town and saw some dejected guys still hoping to be hired, even if only for an hour. But they were probably about to give up. It seems the vineyard owner felt sorry for them, perhaps because they had families or some other reason. Anyway, he hired them as well and told them he would pay them fairly.

The ancient workday was twelve hours, so at six in the evening the vineyard owner called together all those he hired that day and began to pay them from the last he hired to the first. To everyone's surprise, he gave the men he hired at five o'clock a full day's wage. And right down the line—all those who didn't work a full day were given a full day's pay. The part-timers were happy, but as those he hired at six in the morning watched the pay distribution, they were elated. They presumed if the guys who worked only one hour— along with the others who worked less than a full day—all received a full day's wage, they should certainly receive more since they had worked the entire day. But when the vineyard owner came to them, as they agreed, he gave them a day's wage. And they started to complain.

The vineyard owner's response was, "What is your problem? I did not do you wrong. Didn't I pay you exactly what I said I would? The issue is that you are angry with me because I am merciful."

Jesus told this parable because He wanted to describe the Pharisees' lack of understanding (even intolerance) for God's grace. Not only did they not understand it—it infuriated them. How dare Jesus suggest that these sinners He was hanging around, who were drunkards and adulterers and who stole money and cheated their own countrymen, could access God's mercy while they had earned it through effort, sacrifice, and deeds.

That is the good news about grace. It's not fair. If things were fair, we would all be in serious trouble because God would give us exactly what we deserved.

Jesus could be around sinners because His knowledge of their spiritual condition gave Him the ability to accept them with very low expectations concerning their ability to perform spiritually. He was able to love them and accept them in spite of their degenerated spiritual condition. It was a function of His grace.

For people, understanding God's grace is a big enough leap; but to demonstrate it requires Olympic long-jump capabilities. To do both, one must jump a "Grand Canyon sized" gulf filled with rules, regulations, stipulations, and traditions. The process must begin by one first experiencing God's grace for oneself.

God's grace *is not*:

- God's universal mass acceptance of everyone into His kingdom, regardless of what they have done.

- God's overlooking the little sins in our lives because we've not engaged in the major ones.

- God's including those in His kingdom who do not compare in unrighteousness to the criminals in prison.

- God's canceling our bad deeds because we have offset them with good ones.

- God's grading on the curve—in other words, God sees that we are *all* pretty bad, so He lowers the passing criteria to ensure that only the worst are left out.

The extension of God's grace to anyone is based on very strict criteria.

First, we must *realize* we are sinners—disgusting and repulsive sinners. We must come to the place where we fully understand we do not deserve God's forgiveness, nor do we deserve to be a part of God's family. This mindset cannot be overlooked. We must fully acknowledge that we don't deserve God's favor before we can ever receive God's favor. That is why *grace* is defined as "unmerited favor."

Next, we must *recognize* that Jesus' perfect life, and therefore His perfect sacrifice on the cross, is God's only provision for the cleansing of our sinfulness. And the salvation He gives is offered to us as a *free gift* from God because that is the only way we could ever obtain it. His perfection is what caused God to be able to overlook our imperfection and offer salvation freely to us. We cannot acquire it by any other means; efforts, deeds, by way of reason, or otherwise. A gift from God's grace is the only means by which we can obtain it.

Last, in order for Him to make this kind of offering to us sinful and disgusting human beings, we must *receive* God's free gift of salvation with absolute awareness of the immense love that exists for us in the heart of this holy God. That's what is meant in Romans 8:35–39 in the description of the vastness of God's love. It is so vast He even loves us in all of our sin, our rejection of Him, and our shame toward Him. Yet God's grace finds a way to approve of us.

That's grace: favor we have done nothing to earn.

Those are pretty tough criteria, aren't they? It is hard to go to the place where we have such a low opinion of ourselves and of our sinful condition. Yet, this is where we must go mentally and spiritually if we are to acquire God's free gift of eternal life. The good news is that once we cross the line of faith by following these guidelines, we find out how special we actually are to God. We find out that we are actually His one true treasure. And discovering this only increases our appreciation for His grace.

If we don't experience this grace for ourselves, we can never understand it or demonstrate it toward others. More importantly, we can never contribute to an environment of grace where we *walk* or where we *worship*. We will always bring judgment along with us. We will always expect more from people spiritually than they are able to give. Our very lack of understanding will foster an environment of guilt and spiritual inadequacy in people's hearts. We will always be contributing to ugliness instead of beauty in the environment of His church. And people will be repelled by it.

There is a remarkable story illustrating some of the components of God's grace.

One day Jesus was invited to a Pharisee's house by the name of Simon. (See Luke 7:36–50.) While Jesus was there, a notorious sinner (a lady, probably a prostitute) came in and was appealing to Jesus' favor by crying in repentance as she washed and kissed His feet and dried them with her hair. As he watched, Simon was thinking like a typical Pharisee, "If Jesus were really God, He would know how sinful this woman is and not allow her to get near to Him." What Simon didn't realize was Jesus' willingness to allow her to do what she was doing was indicative both of His discernment of her sinful condition and that He was indeed from God. That is what truly godly people would do, because God loves sinners.

Jesus also discerned Simon's thoughts and asked him a question in parable form.

"If two people owed a man money; one fifty days' worth of wages and the other five hundred, if the man forgave both, who would love him more?"

Simon answered, "I suppose the one who was forgiven the most."

Jesus said, "You have answered correctly."

Then, Jesus went on to show how the woman's love for God was greater than Simon's, because her sins were more than Simon's.

There is a phenomenon in Christendom that is universal. No matter how many sins we are forgiven, we are all just as sinful. If I have run the gamut with my sinfulness: lying, cheating, hating, murdering, adulterating, robbing, pillaging, cussing, and coveting; and if you have done nothing worse than pout when your parents said no to you, I am not any more a sinner than you are. We are both equally sinful sinners in need of God's grace. And if we don't appropriate all of the vastness of His grace, neither of us will qualify to be a child of God.

Furthermore, if you don't realize the depth of your sinfulness, even though you have sinned much less than I, you will never appreciate God's grace as much as I do. And you will have a difficult time demonstrating God's grace to others who have committed more sinful deeds than you.

This was made very clear to me when I was introduced to a church made up largely of families whose children grew up and remained in the church in which they were raised. It seemed that a fair percentage of the people had not gone down prodigal paths. Consequently, the church was filled with people who had sinned little. The result was that the church as a whole was not overly tolerant of sinners frequenting their services. All of their church rules were designed to emphasize adherence to a strict set of stipulations rather than grace. They were more "letter of the law people" than they were "merchants of mercy." And their love for God was more defined by how obedient they were to their rules than by their love and acceptance of people less pristine than they.

Let me repeat: in spite of how much or little we have sinned before we come to God, we all need the full expression of God's grace to get into His kingdom. You see, we aren't sinners because we sin. We sin because we are sinners. (See Romans 3:23.) And we are all equally sinful sinners in need of the maximum provision of God's grace. Unless we realize the depth of our sin, we will not be able to contribute to an environment of grace—neither in our own hearts, nor in the atmosphere of our church.

There is another concern that arises. It is one thing to be patient with people who haven't yet crossed the line of faith; but what about those who have given their hearts to Christ but are still living in sinful ways? Should we immediately inform them of the compromising lifestyle they are practicing and press them to change? Or should we let Jesus do that?

You have already heard my view on the issue, but let me rave on by giving you a little more clarity on the topic.

Felicia was a beautiful girl. She was actually the billboard model for a prominent whiskey company. She showed up in our church one Sunday and gave her heart to God. It was a heartfelt conversion and without a doubt, Jesus became her Savior that day.

However, there were some significant barriers standing in the way of her making Him her Lord.

First, though she felt her modeling career with a whiskey company was an awkward profession for a Christian, it brought in money she needed to meet her expenses. And financially she wasn't prepared to give it up. Second, she was living with a man whom she had grown to depend on because of a sense of order he brought to her life. Third, he owned the home and the car she drove. If she left him, she would have no place to live and no transportation. Fourth, he was her contact for her job as a model. If she left him, she would lose her job and her connections to the profession. And, fifth, her son from a previous relationship was a severe epileptic and required institutionalization. It was extremely expensive, and the man she was living with was paying for that expense.

Felicia had become so entwined with a lifestyle that seemed to be holding her captive, she didn't know how to leave it. She counseled with me several times in an effort to try and make the break, which I was encouraging her to do. But in the end she wasn't able. She concluded that in her situation, Christianity was just too difficult for her to embrace. She felt she didn't measure up to the standards our church and what my counsel was asking of her. Felicia was one of the ones I had made grace-mistakes with. Fortunately, I learned. Unfortunately, Felicia paid a dear price for my mistakes.

I always felt, what if I had not pushed so hard? What if I had made her feel more welcome and accepted in spite of her lifestyle? Perhaps she would have stayed in our church long enough to grow in the Lord and hear His voice and His plan to rearrange her life. Certainly His plan would have been a better one than mine. And perhaps by then she would have been strong enough in the Lord to make the break.

Since this incident and through watching many other similar situations after that, I realized that God's salvation is appropriated to different people in different ways and in different time frames. For some, changes are immediate. For others, it takes more time for the power of transformation to take hold. And yet for others, sin has so ensnared them that it takes more than time. It takes time plus awareness, growth, strength, courage, and more. And all the while these qualities are developing in them, it takes grace for us to wait, grace for us to be patient, grace for understanding, and grace to accept them just as they are while they "*grow* in the grace and knowledge" of the Lord Jesus (2 Pet. 3:18).

Grace isn't just a pre-salvation issue. Grace is an all-salvation issue. Since salvation is a life process to be worked out over our entire lives (see Philippians 2:12), it needs to be shown by all of us, to all of us, for the duration of our lives as we walk with the Lord on this earth.

And stunning in beauty is the place where God's grace is felt and shared. Even when it becomes necessary to address issues that may be damaging to individuals who are continuing to live destructive lives of sin, there is a beauty that manifests itself in the environment that knows how to do so in God's grace.

Chapter 3

⁓

Imperfect Christianity

Have you ever wondered what Jesus' words meant, "You will be my witnesses" (Acts 1:8, NIV)?

Frankly, I have lived my whole Christian life—almost forty years—and still I marvel that Christians don't really know what to do with this verse. They don't know what it means to be a witness.

Some television preachers think it means they are supposed to raise money in their church, so they can put their church services on television, so greater numbers of people who don't know Christ can *witness* their people worshipping God over the airwaves.

Some pastors feel it means they need to get out into the community. And so—in the summer months, anyway—they organize a church service in a nearby park with a band, testimonies, a drama, and a sermon. All so outsiders can *witness* their loving of God out in public, and hopefully be enticed to become insiders.

Some Christians think it means they must try to talk to everyone they can, in an attempt to insert communication about Jesus into every conversation they have with people who aren't Christians.

Some feel being a witness means to knock on people's doors and give them a piece of literature, a video, a packet, or an artifact that will inform them of some aspect of the gospel.

Some feel witnessing means to organize a way to serve the community by planning a free car wash, windshield clean, or oil change give-a-way in order to pique an unbeliever's interest in a church that would be so generous.

Some feel witnessing is serving the local school system, helping agencies, or assisting with needs in their community in an effort to show Christ's love.

Some of these...all of these...or in some cases...none of these are what Jesus meant when He said, "Be my witnesses."

I remember in my first pastorate, we would have "Church in the Park" at least one time every summer. The park was right across the street from our church, and every Sunday it would be filled with people. We would lug tables, chairs, guitars, literature, and other paraphernalia across the street and into the center of the park, set up and proceed to hold church.

We would sing our liveliest and most fun songs. We would try to talk and sing extra loud so that people in nearby areas would hear and perhaps, out of curiosity, wander over and check out what we were doing. Now and then I would look up and see a passer-by or a family picnicking at a nearby table, standing on the outskirts of our group taking in what we were doing. Every once in a while, I would see some of our people talking with curiosity seekers, answering questions, socializing, and pointing in the direction of our church as if they were telling them, "We meet at that building over there every Sunday at nine and eleven."

When the service was over, we would eat lunch and play a little softball, after which we would pack up all of our equipment and tote it back to the church.

That was our church's annual stab at witnessing for Christ.

I'm not saying it wasn't witnessing or that Jesus didn't approve. As to whether or not we accomplished what we were trying to do, it's hard to say. I *am* saying, I'm not sure that many of us have stopped to try and understand just what Jesus meant when He said "be witnesses of me."

One idea that Christians, pastors, and churches all over our world have is this: witnessing is letting people who we come in contact with know what a Christian should or shouldn't do. That is, they try to communicate the change Christ has made in their lives by pointing out to people the things He has helped them to stop doing.

This usually starts out innocent enough with a testimony to friends after the convert's miraculous conversion to Christ. And believe me, this is very persuasive—at least in the beginning. This is what Zacchaeus did when Jesus went to his house for a gathering. At a certain point he collected all of his sinner friends together with Jesus and his disciples. Then Zacchaeus quieted all who were present and proclaimed that he had changed his ways—that he was going to give money to the poor and pay back all those he had cheated fourfold. The scripture seems to indicate this made quite an impact.

When I first became a Christian, the change God performed in me was so pronounced I wanted to tell everyone, and I did. But over time, when I would communicate those changes to others, they started sounding more like condemnation than miracles. I used to feel my testimony was best demonstrated when I pointed out the victorious and drastic alterations God had made in my life. I would say, I don't drink anymore. I don't cuss, steal, smoke, or carouse anymore.

But when my initial spiritual honeymoon wore off, this kind of talk sounded more like I was trying to tell them how righteous I was and how unrighteous they were. It's not what I meant, but it's what it sounded like to them. All of the miracles that were involved in my conversion and transformation that sounded so wondrous to people in the beginning gave way to feelings of guilt and an inability for those who heard to measure up. Though my intentions were pure, they felt as if I were saying I was holy, and they weren't. I was righteous, they were dastardly. And they felt as if I were trying to draw extra attention to this dichotomy by talking about it. They went away feeling I was one of those "holier than thou" types.

Then, some people who heard me talk about the changes God had performed in me felt it was fine for me, but they just weren't that kind of person. I was religion-prone, they were not. I had a propensity toward being pious, they didn't. So how could they ever make the leap to where I was? And no amount of convincing would change that. I tried to tell them I wasn't religious either—that I had been just like them before God moved in my life. But it didn't help because spiritual change and transformation were foreign terms to them. It was as if my terminology was coming from another language entirely and there was no term in their language that had the same meaning. So my witnessing about the change in my life at a certain point lost its meaning, and therefore its effectiveness.

Here is what I didn't realize. As my walk with the Lord went along, my focus on the outward things I didn't do anymore was an indication I was making a transition to the pharisaical and judgmental side of Christianity. It was subtle but it was there—even if only slightly. I was beginning to become disgusted with unbelievers because of the way they were living. I began to feel a lack of tolerance and understanding for their inability to understand what I was trying to tell them about God and the change He had accomplished in me. I was beginning to feel my attitude was righteous and holy because God wanted us to live holy lives. Therefore anyone who didn't was out of His will. And they were picking up on this attitude of self-righteousness and judgment. That was early on in my new-found walk with the Lord.

Similarly, at a certain point I went through a phase in my pastoral leadership that focused my outward actions on those of the people I was leading. I found myself zeroing in on the little sins I would catch people doing. If they cussed by accident, I would shake my finger at them. If I saw them in a public place smoking a cigarette, I would scold them. If I caught them laughing at an off-color joke, I would shake my head in disappointment.

Furthermore, from the pulpit I would talk favorably about the perfect and pious actions of Christianity being the only acceptable behaviors in our Lord's eyes—and pooh pooh all of the imperfect actions I had seen in people. I would find myself not being totally honest about my own failures as a Christian, because I was beginning to feel that "perfect Christianity" was what "being a witness" for Christ was all about. If people knew I wasn't perfect, they wouldn't trust me as their pastor, and they wouldn't have an adequate example to follow. If they didn't have that from me, how could they be perfect, and how could they and our church be witnesses for Jesus? After all, being a witness meant being a perfect Christian.

Let me clarify—I knew I wasn't perfect, and they knew it as well. But that is the fallacy of the idea that "being perfect" has the same meaning as "being a witness." It was an impossible objective and made everyone feel inadequate. No one is being a witness for Christ by trying to put on a perfect front.

Unwittingly I was creating an environment that alienated most of the people in my church. They weren't feeling that they should change their ways to be better. They were feeling that they could never measure up.

I have learned over the years, people don't need anyone to say anything in order for them to feel condemned and judged. All they need is someone who is living a more holy life than they to merely stand next to them and carry on normal conversation. If someone more righteous than you sits with you over coffee, they don't need to tell you that you are living poorly and they are living righteously. You'll know it. If they merely sit with you, you will feel less righteous than they.

In the same vein, if you are a victorious Christian, and you stand next to an unbeliever for any length of time and just carry on normal communication, not only will that unbeliever feel inadequate spiritually, he or she will begin to feel judged by you. You haven't said a word of judgment, but they feel it just the same. That is the power of righteous living. That unbeliever may even talk to others about how judgmental you are, even if you never said a word of condemnation to them.

Once when I was a very young youth pastor, I went to a summer camp with my youth group. One of the speakers dealt with the evils of the tongue. As he spoke, I began to feel convicted about the loose and destructive talk I was allowing to come from my mouth. Later that day I was walking with a friend and the speaker walked by. My friend knew the speaker so he stopped him and introduced him to me. As I shook his hand, I began to feel an incredible weight of condemnation. I felt dirty, as if I were the worst sinner and gossip in the world. I felt like the speaker could discern my every shortcoming with regard to my tongue. Yet, he never said anything condemning. He was a great guy. I felt all that just standing next to him. Some non-Christians will feel condemned just from standing next to a Christian; that Christian may not have to say a thing.

Here is the reason. As much as humans want to suggest they are impervious to sin and do not feel guilty about their sinful behavior, the fact is people are very sensitive about their indiscretions and sinful condition before God and in front of people. That is why people search high and low for some form of religious ritual, sect, or practice that will give them some relief from the guilt they feel from their sin. And that is why people will invent elaborate rationalizations for sinful behavior like: citing their moral accomplishments, ethical comparisons, and idealisms. That is also why people will go to the mat over their moral condition in utter denial that they are sinners, that their lifestyle is sinful, or even that the indiscretion they may have recently committed was a sin.

It is all because people are incredibly sensitive about their sinfulness, bringing credence to the Bible's claim that "all have sinned and have fallen short of the glory of God" (Rom. 3:23).

It is also why churches, pastors, and Christians who expect perfection from people as a "witness" for Christ will create an environment that feels like futility and one that fosters frustration in people. It is uncomfortable. It is pharisaical. It is not one that reflects Jesus' aspirations for his church and its members. It is what Jesus challenged for three years non-stop with the religious leaders.

If perfect Christianity is your idea of witnessing, you will be endlessly disappointed and largely ineffective.

What does "being a witness" actually mean?

As I observe scripture, not just this single phrase in Acts 1:8, but taking all the verses I see in the New Testament, and even a few in the Old that have to do with witnessing; this is what I believe it means: a little talking, a little living, and a whole lot of "being."

I'm sure you have heard the expression "talk is cheap."

I have observed over the years, whether in church or in life, that those who talk the loudest and the longest are probably the furthest from whatever virtuosity they are trying to communicate with their talk. That is why they talk. They want to draw attention to their virtue because people may not be able to detect it otherwise.

But what about living—shouldn't living something out be a good way to witness? Yes, but living something out doesn't necessarily mean it is a functioning part of that person's whole life.

Exercising is a great example. Let's say a person decides he is going to change his exercise routine around the first of the year. So he starts to run every morning. For a week or two or three, he will run, pump weights, eat properly, and so forth. Often he will also talk about how it is changing his life, how good he feels, how energetic he seems, how productive he has become. And you may be convinced that he is a changed person because after all—he is "living out" his commitment. He is "walking his talk," so to speak. But if you were to follow him around for six weeks or so, you may find him starting to slack off. He doesn't run every day anymore, and he has started to decline in his weight lifting. Then, in eight weeks he is finished. But for all practical purposes he seemed to be "living it out."

I can't count the times I have encountered Christians who seemed to be living out their faith, only to be disappointed as I watched them drop the whole thing a few months later.

No, Jesus said, "Be my witnesses." He didn't say talk witness talk. He didn't even say live like a witness. He said, "Be my witnesses." He was telling us: allow Me to become so a part of your lives that you reflect My glory without even trying. You see, at a certain point, living it gives way to "being it."

Having said this, here is my point. Perfect Christianity is not an authentic witness because there are no perfect Christians. Not one! Consequently, this interpretation of being a witness is bogus. It rings of pharisaical trappings and fails to understand the whole idea of how to "bear witness" of Christ (John 15:27).

So what is it? What is being a witness of Christ? I believe it is being the imperfect Christian you are, being the imperfect pastor you are, being the imperfect church you are. It is far more authentic, honest, effective, and pleasing to God for believers to be flawed and blemished, and yet genuinely devoted to Christ, than to appear to be a perfect, victorious, pristine, and shiny Christian—and not be anything of the kind.

Pastors, be honest about your failures, shortcomings, and inconsistencies from the pulpit. To be honest doesn't mean you need to hang out your dirty laundry for all to see. Wise pastors can discern the difference. But the honesty climate of a church is usually set by its leaders. If the leaders are honest, it cultivates an environment of honesty that will filter throughout the whole fellowship. It is a breath of fresh air that will cause the constituency to breathe deeply and feel at liberty to be open and honest about their shortcomings. It's beautiful. But it doesn't stop there.

The real place of effective witnessing isn't anywhere near the church walls. It is out in the world where lost people live and have their existence. Can you "be" a completely honest witness of Christ with the unbelievers in your daily routine?

Let me tell you Rob's story.

Rob was a business owner in Boulder, Colorado. The business he owned was a music store and every musician in town knew Rob. So did the majority of the pastors. Most of the churches in town went to Rob for their music and sound needs. And just about every evangelical pastor in town would try to share with Rob about the faith.

Rob's mother was an atheist and brought Rob up to believe the same. Consequently, Rob was Buddhist, New Age, atheist, or something—or nothing. No one was quite sure and neither was Rob. But Rob's wife was a non-practicing Catholic.

Rob did appreciate the business all the evangelical churches in town gave him. And it was a lot. Boulder, Colorado, is a very un-churched community, as well as a beautiful and weather-friendly place to live. A steady stream of church-planting pastors come into Boulder in hopes of starting and establishing a successful church there. It seemed that most of them went to Rob for their sound and music needs. Rob would give them each a great deal, and most would try to witness to Rob. With each he was uninterested, but he did appreciate their business and felt strongly that the key reason his business started becoming successful was because of the many evangelical churches that came to Boulder to try to make a go of it.

I was one of those pastors. I too came to the beautiful Colorado city because I felt God had called me there to plant a church. And when it came time to purchase sound and music equipment, like the many pastors before and after me, I went to Rob's music store.

Rob was such a nice guy. He had the ability to give you the impression that he was your best friend. That is probably why he was such a good salesman. I fell for the aura of friendship he radiated and developed the idea that Rob kind of liked me—and maybe he did, a little anyway. I found out that Rob liked to play golf, so I would bring up the subject as often as I could without feeling awkward. He never seemed to bite, though. He would always respond, "Yeah we should go some time." But I never felt he was really interested.

One day as he helped me carry some boxes to my car, he confronted me about a spiritual issue. There in his parking lot he got into a heated altercation with me about the Christian perspective that "Jesus is the only way to Heaven." I wasn't sure why he felt compelled to go at me the way he did, or why he chose me. But I didn't wince. I came right back at him. And in a bit of a skirmish, we had it out—right there in front of my car.

In trying to soften the discomfort we were feeling, I concluded the conversation by saying, "I've got an idea. Let's get together and play a round of golf—just for fun."

That was the beginning of my relationship with Rob C.

We started playing now and then, and soon we had a weekly golf date on the calendar. This went on for three years with periodic interruptions from inclement weather during the winter months. Sometimes we would talk about God. Sometimes we wouldn't. Sometimes we would just play golf. But at a certain point a real trust began to form between Rob and me. He began to feel free to share some of his frustrations; frustrations with his business, customers, or his kid's coaches. And I would do the same with him.

While my wife and I were in Boulder, we had many challenges. I found myself sharing some of my frustrations as a father, a pastor, and a Christian. I even shared some of my discomfort with issues that arose in my church.

At earlier times in my ministry, I would have felt it was a poor witness to share those kinds of things with someone like Rob. My feeling was that talking about those kinds of things would cause someone like him to think I wasn't a very good witness of Christianity. My thinking was that a person would not have been attracted to Christianity if he or she knew Christians have some severe problems and challenges too. Or maybe I thought that in his limited understanding of Christianity, he would have wondered if God had it out for me, that I wasn't a good reflection of God's image, or it would diminish his trust that God really had the power to change lives.

But that was before—I didn't feel that way when I was building my relationship with Rob.

So I shared the truth. It wasn't ugly. I didn't portray any bitterness I may have felt toward people and God. I was just honest. I was merely being exactly who I was, a Christian who loved God and who had problems. I was being the "imperfect Christian" I was, and I was being honest about it.

Now, make no mistake about it, I maintained my testimony. I didn't cuss in front of Rob because I don't do that in public or private; not when I hit a bad shot on the golf course or when I am frustrated in life. And I didn't drink in front of Rob. I've already told you about the decision I made concerning drinking early on in my Christian life. Nor did I bad-mouth people or leadership. I didn't gossip or cheat or steal. I maintained integrity in those areas because that is who I am. So my testimony remained intact, and Rob noticed it. I never had to draw attention to it. He just noticed it.

And there was something else; we grew to be genuine friends. He knew I felt that he was more than just my golfing partner. He was my friend, and I was his. I accepted him the way he was in all of his sin—foul language, political opinions, attitudes, and shortcomings. I didn't judge him for any of them. I just listened and loved him anyway.

Recently, my wife and I had dinner with Rob and his wife, Jeanne. Jeanne shared with my wife that her husband had experienced a spiritual awakening in his life. He used to be an atheist, but now believed God does exist. She shared that she knew the change in Rob was due to his relationship with me.

She said to Shirley, "It seemed every minister that came to Boulder and bought equipment from Rob tried to convert him to Christianity. But when Rob started playing golf with Chris, it was different. Chris was Rob's friend. This gave Rob the opportunity to see Chris was genuine; he truly believed what he lived, and lived it every day. But Chris never made Rob feel as if he didn't measure up. He made God's existence believable for Rob."

Jeanne also told us that the change in Rob had helped her to feel free to lean back in the direction of her spiritual roots, which was the Catholic Church.

Rob still isn't a Christian, but his belief in God has been awakened, and he trusts Christians again. I moved away from the Boulder area before I was able to see him bow his knee to Christ, but I suspect it will only be a matter of time before Rob steps over the line of faith.

What kind of witness are you emanating in your walk, your ministry, your church?

It is a continuous breath of fresh air to be able to simply "be" who God made you to be—with all of your warts, problems, pitfalls, failures, blemishes, and sins.

Here's another expression you have probably heard. "He is comfortable in his own skin." It is the proclamation of the true witness of Christianity. To be able to walk confidently, humbly, and yet peacefully down any walkway, roadway, hallway, or fairway knowing you are in right standing with God and man. You are the same person in public that you are in private. You can be transparent with people because you know God is OK with who you are—and therefore you are OK with who you are, and if people aren't OK with that, it's still OK with you. It is just the joy of being honest with yourself, God, and others about who you are.

For your information, this kind of peace with self begins with personal prayer; and in that prayer, being honest with God about your sins and shortcomings as often as you can. In time you will learn experientially that God is OK with you.

When a Christian, a church leader, or a church radiates this kind of honesty, it is beautiful. It is like walking into a gathering where you are the guest of honor. You feel accepted and approved of no matter what you have done. You can be open and honest and display all of your spiritual warts and blemishes if you want to, regardless of how repulsive they may be.

Imperfect Christianity is "true" Christianity because there are no perfect Christians. Perfect Christianity is a fallacy.

I have also found that when judgementalism and perfect expectations are absent, the pressure departs for people to measure up. When this happens, people's desire to seek the approval of men fades, and their desire to find the approval of

God increases. They are free to listen to the still small voice in their own soul from the Holy Spirit who is trying to speak to them about their sin. So that when they respond, they are responding to the pleasure of God and not men. That is most beautiful of all.

Chapter 4

~

Fun and Laughter

NOT LONG AGO I spoke in a church in Colorado. I communicated a message I had spoken in other places before; one that was heavy on my heart and one that was contained in my books. But this time it had a different effect. The mood was intense. I had spoken passionately and forcefully. The people were noticeably impacted and the pastor was weeping. As I concluded, I handed the service back over to him, and he seemed to be at a loss for words. When he finally spoke, it was obvious he was trying to offer support for the message I had just delivered, but his words were awkward. At the end of his first short phrase, there was a chuckle that went through the room. He spoke again in support, but it was clear he was still awkward because he had been moved emotionally. The mood seemed to demand seriousness, but when he spoke his next words again a chuckle went through the crowd. But this time it was louder and longer. It seemed that with each phrase he spoke, though the mood was serious, the people wanted to laugh and kept doing so until the pastor suggested he was trying to be serious.

What was going on there?

The crowd needed comic relief. It seemed that the sermon I had delivered was moving and solicited a serious response, but their emotions had had enough seriousness; and by the end of my message needed laughter.

Those familiar with literature and the stage know that playwrights and novelists use comic relief because they are aware their audience needs a reprieve when they have been overwhelmed with sadness and seriousness in the course of a story.

How much more do humans who are overwhelmed with the sadness and despair of life in all of its reality need to find reason to laugh, have fun, express their joy, and be happy?

Here is the Bible's take on this. "A merry heart does good, like medicine" (Prov. 17:22). Lest I communicate that mere laughing at jokes is what I am talking about, let me clarify. Laughter, for the one who believes in God, has a deeper source than much of the laughter that happens at the hands of famous comics and joke-tellers in our world.

As Jesus pointed out in His Sermon on the Mount in Matthew 5:7, personal joy is better than mere laughter. He defines a merry heart in the beginning of this particular sermon as one that is blessed. And with eight descriptions of a contrite spirit, He identifies the source of true happiness and a merry heart.

The most important ingredient to an environment of fun and laughter is permission. Do people you lead have permission to have fun? I have been around people and in churches where they didn't. In these churches, basic attitudes or persuasions prevailed that made people feel laughter was not particularly sanctioned. They felt, for example that frivolity equals a lack of spirituality, happiness is strictly within and shouldn't be expressed by emotions, or the Bible makes little or no mention of laughter so we probably shouldn't do much of it in the church.

Believe it or not there are quantities of people who truly believe that lightheartedness and laughter in a ministry setting don't mix. They feel that ministry and laughter together, is an oxymoron. Warren Jeffs, the leader of a splinter cult group from the Mormon Church meeting in Southwest Colorado, reportedly made laughter a sin and forbade it among his followers. He was captured and arrested on polygamy and child abuse charges in 2006; but his same controlling tendencies have seemed to capture the ministry mindsets of many well-meaning evangelical leaders, because they fear its presence in their churches. They don't forbid laughter and fun altogether, but they are afraid to allow much of it to go on.

We've all met people who in the presence of comedy refuse to laugh. To be fair, some people may not get the joke. It goes over their heads like a 747 goes over the ocean blue. I've had naïve moments myself. But some people make a conscious and instantaneous decision to not laugh at a joke for spiritual purposes. That is, they feel if they laugh at an off-color joke, their laughter will communicate a poor testimony of Christ. Will it?

I have actually been in situations where people outside the faith have told off-color jokes to test me. They wanted to see if they could arouse a smile on my face in an effort to prove that I was as susceptible to the temptations of the flesh as they were. I have a news flash: I am as susceptible as the next person. But I do have a pat way of reacting to these kinds of moments. My response to these comedic occasions may not be popular, but it's what I do. My response is usually a light chuckle and a shake of my head aimed more at the teller than the joke.

In this response I am trying to communicate four things. 1) I got the joke. I am not a monk isolated off in some remote desert somewhere incapable of understanding the real world. 2) I discerned their intent to test me. I'm not stupid in that regard. 3) I am not disgusted with their attempt at trying to find fun in a questionable joke as a substitute for the unhappiness that I know exists in their hearts. It's what the ungodly do. For many outside of Christ's love, laughing at a questionable joke is the only source of sanity they have in their world of spiritual emptiness and confusion. And, 4) I'm not going to scold them for telling it. I am going to love them anyway. It is what Jesus would do. With these four things in the back of my mind, I keep the environment of fun present when people are around me. I will not communicate to them that Christians can't laugh or have fun because they are already convinced that is so. I want to try to correct their false assumptions.

I have even had people tell me an off-color joke just because they thought it was funny. And then afterward, realizing they had told it to a Christian, they say, "Now you have to admit, that *is* funny."

In my mind, understanding the intent of the joke, I can see the humor. However, deep in my spirit I don't think the joke is funny at all, because I know their funny story is a commentary on the emptiness and sadness they feel in this life without the joy of Christ living in their hearts. But they wouldn't understand it if I tried to communicate all of that to them. They would think me a weird prude and close the door, preventing me from ever talking with them again about matters of faith. So I respond to the joke with my mind, the love of Jesus in my heart, and the character of grace God is trying to form in my life. I smile and say, "You're right. It is funny." That way I keep my relationship with them intact.

That was FYI.

But what I really want to talk about is the kind of atmosphere present among some Christians who choose not to laugh at a joke because they feel laughter and fun are somehow less spiritual than seriousness and piety. There are many Christians and church leaders who feel that permitting laughter and fun is akin to hindering people from receiving from God, because they feel frivolity contradicts spirituality.

I knew one pastor who would allow no staff person to talk from the pulpit about sports, matches, games, players, or scores in either a joking or non-joking way. His reasoning was that God didn't need the fun of sports to get the attention of His people in worship. He was actually a huge sports fan. He just didn't want it in church. I was on his staff, and I cooperated with his point of view, but in theory I disagreed. My feeling is that sports are a joy and a pastime of a huge segment of our world. To not engage people from a sports platform—where so many live—is to communicate that we aren't relevant to their lives and may not approve of their fun.

Jesus didn't specifically address football, baseball, basketball, golf, soccer, or hockey—or for that matter any other sport. But he used every other facet of people's lives to connect with them. He talked about farmers, soldiers, flowers, birds, beaches, trees, fishing, and money. Believe me, if competitive sports had been any part of the people's lives whatsoever, He would have used the subject to connect with them. And most of you probably know that the Apostle Paul did use athletes and athletics in the Bible to illustrate some of his points.

Are people permitted to laugh and yuck it up around you? Do they have your consent to inject the medicine of a merry heart into the environment in your presence? Can you tolerate a joke? Are you able to see that a person can laugh and not lose any points with God?

You may think this an unnecessary discussion because you have no problem with fun and laughter. But bear with me as I address other points in this discussion.

Next, some feel the happiness the Bible refers to should only be felt inwardly. After all, God's word never describes Jesus as laughing or having a smile on His face. This is a prominent opinion in some circles.

In his depiction of the life of Jesus in the motion picture *Gospel Road*, Johnny Cash attempted to dispel what he thought was a myth—that Jesus didn't laugh. The director, maker, financier, and participant in the film had Jesus laughing with His disciples as they walked on the dusty Judean roads together. He depicted Jesus telling funny stories and laughing at the antics of His twelve most intimate followers, putting His arm around them with a big smile on His face and having a good old time with them.

This was one of the first times anyone had ever tried to show Jesus in this light, and frankly, it was shocking to some and liberating to others. When church leaders made reference to the display, it was a point of controversy with many people.

As recently as a few years ago when on the silver screen Mel Gibson presented his astounding rendition of the passion play, he too challenged the opinions of the pious. He portrayed Jesus as a young man making jokes to His mother Mary about His invention of a stool and fun-lovingly splashing water on her. Yes, there is no specific biblical record indicating that Jesus laughed, had fun, or kidded around. But everything that surrounded His actions and teaching indicates He must have.

Jesus said you would be happy when you perform the eight beatitudes. (See Matthew 5.)

He pronounced in Matthew 5:12, the last of His beatitudes, "Rejoice and be exceedingly glad for great is your reward in heaven."

In John 7:38, Jesus said, "He who believes in Me...out of his heart will flow rivers of living water."

Could Jesus tell His followers to be happy and not be happy himself? Could He have been a "do as I say and not as I do" kind of God? Every indication is that Jesus sanctioned fun and laughter. Could Jesus have approved of it for every one of the people He taught, while He Himself was unable to generate a laugh from His own being? I think that opinion undermines the genuineness and transparency—even the holiness—of God Himself. Could God recommend or require an emotional response from people He is not capable of conveying Himself, or one He feels is out of order for Him to express?

There are a couple of scriptures that identify guidelines that help us to know there are boundaries to laughter.

Romans 12:15 says, "Rejoice with those who rejoice, and weep with those who weep." In other words, be ready to cry with those who are hurting. It is a healing and caring aspect of Christianity that must be a part of our walk with Christ. But equally a part of our walk with the Lord should be our ability to celebrate, cheer, rejoice, and laugh with those who have had happy things happen for them. We've all seen jealousy and envy hinder this from happening. But the scripture is saying that a healthy and genuine believer should be ready to cheer and rejoice in the good news that God wills for others.

Another scripture that lays out boundaries regarding laughter is Ecclesiastes 3:4, "There is…A time to weep, And a time to laugh." And Proverbs 25:20 implies that a light heart around a heavy spirit is cruel. These scriptures suggest the issue isn't laughing or crying; the issue is sensitivity to know when to laugh and when to cry.

The third scripture is Ephesians 5:4, "Neither filthiness, nor foolish talking, nor coarse jesting, which are not fitting, but rather giving of thanks." The Living Bible gives what is probably a loose translation of this verse but it may be helpful for us to see it: "Dirty stories, foul talk and coarse jokes—these are not for you. Instead, remind each other of God's goodness and be thankful." I think Christians would agree; laughter that goes along with this kind of communication is outside of the parameters of where believers in Jesus Christ are supposed to live.

However, it is my feeling—theologically speaking—that within these boundaries, laughter and fun is a big YES. Within those boundaries, there ought to be many areas where Christians can laugh hysterically.

One of those areas might be called, "the funny happenings that occur in life." How do you watch a dog chase its tail without laughing at some point? And I'm sorry, clumsiness *is* funny. When people slip, trip, stumble, fall, or plop on their rumps, especially when they are trying to be dignified, it's funny. When a goose chases a man around a park it is worthy of hysterical laughter. And when young men and women try to get together in the thing we call love, the nervousness and awkwardness they feel is flat out hilarious.

When my wife and I first tried to get together, it was a side-splitter.

She saw me leaning over a drinking fountain on a Monday in the high school we both attended. On an impulse, she bopped me over the head with her purse. It was a flirtatious move she would wonder about for decades to come. In response, I wheeled around to see the most beautiful girl I had ever laid eyes on. I knew who she was. Everyone knew who Shirley LaPorte was—only the most gorgeous girl in school. And here she was hitting my head with her purse.

"It had to have been a mistake," I thought. "This school knockout couldn't have possibly aimed her flirt in my direction—on purpose."

"You gonna hog all the water?" she asked with a sassy smile on her face.

I blubbered something I thought was cool—but was actually stupid and nonsensical—and moved out of her way with my mouth open in a full out gawk. She stepped forward, leaned over, took a sip, and walked away with two of her girlfriends at her side.

I wasn't the brightest light in the building, but I was at least smart enough to know I had better not let this opportunity slip away.

The next day I found her and asked if she would like to go to a movie. She turned me down flat, said something about not being able to go. I walked away disappointed and a little baffled. Had I read the bop on the head wrong?

Strike one. But I regrouped.

The next day I found her in the hall by her locker and asked if she would like to go with me to the homecoming dance the weekend coming up. Again she turned me down without a conscience. She couldn't go to the dance either, and I walked away downhearted and even more confused.

Strike two. How could I know she went to a church that thought both of those kinds of dates were sins?

But a second time I regrouped. I knew her class (she was a year older) was working on their float for homecoming right down the street from where my class was working on ours. It wasn't much, but I thought maybe she would consent to a rendezvous.

On Thursday, still riding the hope that her bopping my head on Monday was a flirt and not a fluke, I found her again. This time, however, I was braced for strike three.

I said nervously, "You know...uh...Friday night...uh... I hear that your class is working on your float at Megan's house....Uh...my class is working on our float at Kyle's house...and they are just down the street from each other. Are you going to help with your float?"

She answered, "I was thinking about it. Why?"

I said, "Well...I was going to help...and I was thinking...you know...if you were going...you know...we could meet."

Such poise—such grace—such eloquence!

Now, I never went to those kinds of things. I didn't have great amounts of class loyalty or spirit when it came to activities like float-making. But I figured this was no time to revert to old habits.

To my surprise Shirley responded, "Um...OK...I guess we could meet."

On the outside I tried to act in control, but inside I was doing flips—more accurately, flipping out. It wasn't a grand slam. It wasn't even a homerun, a triple, a double, or even a single. It was barely a walk from being hit by a pitch. But at least it wasn't a strikeout.

The next evening, Friday night, we were to meet outside one of the predetermined houses. I wore my favorite shirt and shorts. They clashed but I didn't know. I brought a friendship ring with me which I had purchased right after school the day before. My intention was that at just the right moment, I would ask her to go steady. I know it was a bit soon, but I figured this was no time to play it cool. I needed to act fast—before she came to her senses.

When I arrived at the designated rendezvous point, she was there. We walked and talked for a while. At a certain point it was time for the kiss. I wasn't nervous, I was frantic. We were standing alone in Kyle's front yard beside a large pine tree. It had just gotten dark. All was quiet, peaceful, romantic. I stepped forward to embrace her and plant the momentous kiss on her lips. As I stepped, however, my foot found a rut in the lawn. I put my full weight on my forward foot and my ankle turned. My immediate romantic reaction was to grasp my injured ankle, pull it up behind me, and start jumping on one foot in a circle in front of Shirley as I screamed in pain.

My reluctant date watched in horror as I hopped around in front of her like a deranged kangaroo. Her horror was not that I was in pain, but that she had actually gone through with the head-bop four days earlier. The event in front of the drinking fountain flashed before her eyes and she thought, "What have I done? I had a split second where I could have stopped myself. Why didn't I?" And as she stood there that Friday night of October in 1966, unable to believe her eyes as I pranced before her in pain, pity entered her heart.

We've been married almost forty years at the time of this writing. It is a miracle equivalent to the Red Sea's parting that we ever got together.

Christians ought to be able to laugh at the funny circumstances in life.

Christians, churches, and leaders of churches should also be able to laugh at themselves. It is reminiscent of a kind of maturity and a healthy self image that reflects a safe environment for people to grow in.

There was once a person on our staff who seemed to radiate a fun-loving personality. My wife and a few others thought it might be a hoot to have a party for him on his upcoming birthday and put together a video of some of his antics we had captured over the months on film. They had a blast putting it together, but when the event finally arrived and they showed the video clips, it was a disaster.

We watched the man's countenance drop lower and lower as the images and jokes were presented. It wasn't cruel, not at all a roast. It was just a fun-hearted friendly spoof. But he never recovered. He puttered around the rest of the party and left early.

From then on we were reluctant to kid with him about anything. Soon after that we learned he had some other severe issues in his life. His inability to take a joke and laugh at himself was an indication of a lacking in emotional health. Such is the case with any Christian and church leader. Our inability to laugh at ourselves is a suggestion of emotional ill-health and unwholesome pride. But its opposite is also true. When someone is able to laugh at and kid about his or her shortcomings, it creates freedom. People are able to identify and accept their own blemishes with less condemnation and fewer feelings of failure.

In the first church I led as senior pastor, we hired a couple we knew from Bible college to work as administrators and worship leaders. Jim Stamp and his wife Jan have been great friends over the years and after they left our church, eventually they began to pastor their own gathering of believers. Recently Jim asked me to be a guest speaker at his church, and I told them a story about Jim. It was a little embarrassing, but Jim took it as the mature man he is.

One Easter we were going to put on a forty-five-minute-long cantata. It was still a time when cantatas and choir robes were the going thing, and Jim wanted the program to start off with a bang. His plan was to begin the event by turning on the lights. And, at the precise time the lights would come on, the choir would be in place and would begin their first number, powerfully and impressively.

We had put black paper in all the windows to ensure no light would enter. We made sure no light could come in through the rear doors by covering up every door window and every crack that could allow light to enter through them.

As people arrived in the sanctuary, naturally we left lights on so people could see to enter and visit as the time neared for the performance to start.

By the time we were ready to begin, the church was packed to the brim. Every seat was filled; I mean every seat. And we had put extra rows in the back and the center aisle to contain the crowds. And they were all filled. We also put two rows of seats along the side walls in the front of the church, and they were filled as well.

Our church was configured such that behind the platform and to either side were offices with doors that opened to the sanctuary on either side of the platform. These doors opened in front of the two rows of chairs we had put on the side walls in the front of the sanctuary.

Jim's plan was to have the choir in one of the rear offices. When the sanctuary lights went out, the choir would shut the light in the office where they were waiting. Then they would file out in the dark, in front of the two rows we had added. They would turn to the left in front of the first row to the center of the church, go up the platform, and be in place ready to start singing the second the lights came on.

However, there were a few factors he had not foreseen. First, Jim didn't realize how limited the walk areas would be if the church was packed. Second, he had not anticipated how blind each member of the choir would be the second the lights went out.

As we planned, as soon as the lights went out in the sanctuary the lights also went out in the back room, at which time the door was opened. It was so dark you could feel the darkness and the choir's ability to see was non-existent. Just the same, the choir began to file into the sanctuary. Because of the crowded conditions, which the choir could not see, they found themselves stepping on the feet and tripping over the ankles of the people sitting in the side rows. You could hear painful responses as feet were being stepped on and toes were being crushed. In addition, you could hear choir members saying softly, "Excuse me... I'm sorry," or cries of embarrassment as they stumbled into the laps of the audience. This awkwardness continued to occur as the choir filed past the two side rows and around in front of those sitting in the first row.

The last in line was Jim, the choir director. He also took part in the abusive display by tripping over someone's ankle, falling into a lady's lap, and accidentally grabbing her knee to keep from tumbling all the way to the floor. When he grabbed her knee, she uttered a short scream characteristic of a woman being surprised by forward and intimate contact.

To make matters worse, the packed crowd, realizing what was happening, began to be amused by the debacle they sensed and heard happening but could not see. A chuckle had begun to filter through the audience in an attempt to annihilate our serious and powerful beginning. And the choir was being drawn into the ever-rising laughter as well.

To top it off, Jim had established a position toward the front of the church in the center aisle from which he would lead the choir. He had a stool there with a music stand in front of it, and in the dark it was his destination. His plan was when he reached it, he would give the word, the lights would come on, and he would begin with a bang. However, when the lights actually came on and the choir looked down at their director, it was hard for them to take him seriously. Jim's hair was violently disheveled. His choir robe stole around his neck was completely out of place, and his glasses were cockeyed on his face. As the lights came on revealing Jim's comical appearance, the entire choir began to laugh at the hilarious sight. I stepped up and tried to bring seriousness back to the moment, but our powerful beginning was gone. As I told the story about Jim, he laughed right along with his church.

Laughing at our mistakes and weaknesses is a sign of health and an example to folks that we are flawed, but it's OK. It is an indication that humility exists in our hearts concerning our frailty, which unleashes God's favor and power and releases Him to lift us up. (See James 4:10.)

Another area where fun and laughter should be able to occur is in bloopers. A slip of the tongue, a mispronunciation, a double meaning can always provoke a laugh.

Pastor Don was doing a double baby dedication. He invited two couples up onto the platform with their new babies. For one couple, it was their first child; for the other, it was their fifth. It was this pastor's practice when he did baby dedications to ask the parents to bring their whole family with them onto the platform for the ceremony. So on one side of Pastor Don stood the couple with their one newborn in Mom's arms, and on the other side stood the other couple with their four children standing in front of them and their baby in Mom's arms. That day Pastor Don read the scripture out of Psalms 127:3–5. It goes like this, "Behold, children are a heritage from the Lord. The fruit of the womb is *His* reward. Like arrows in the hand of a warrior, So are the children of one's youth. Happy is the man who has his quiver full of them."

No one knows why Pastor Don spoke his next words, but he would spend the next several years living them down. After he read verse five, he looked at the couple with one baby and then at the family with five children and said to the church, "Of course, as you can see, some men have bigger quivers than others."

The service was over. There were other segments to complete and a sermon to deliver, but everything was anti-climactic after that.

One Sunday morning I was leading worship at the church I was pastoring. During rehearsal before church, we determined our keyboard player, whose name was Paul, would be the one to play the introduction for one of our worship songs, a beautiful tune about our love for God entitled

"You're the Love of My Life." When it came time to sing the song in the service, Paul forgot that he was supposed to begin the song. Certain it was his responsibility to do the intro, I looked over at him as if waiting for him to start. When I looked at him, Paul thought I had spaced and had not begun because I wasn't sure what the next song was supposed to be.

So to help me out, he said, "Pastor Chris, "You're the Love of My Life."

I looked back at him and said, "Well, I love you too Paul. But should we be talking about that in front of all these people?"

Our church laughed for nearly ten minutes before we could go on.

There is wholesome and joyous fun that can happen in Christ if leaders will foster an environment that gives people permission to laugh and have fun in the Lord.

The world is filled with laughter that is corrupt, that soils the heart and stains the conscience of those who engage in its humor. How clean it feels to laugh at things that are truly funny in an environment that is pure and holy, and to experience no guilt for doing so.

Before my wife and I came to Christ, we had spent several months trying to build a relationship with some friends, especially one couple we knew growing up. These friends enjoyed drinking and carousing, and we were quite convinced we enjoyed that kind of lifestyle as well. But the last several times we were with them, they drank too much, got into a fight with each other, or got into a fight with us.

Around the same time, a couple in the church we were connected with asked us to do things with them. A few times we spent the whole day with this couple, in addition to three or four evenings. And we had a blast.

I well-remember analyzing and comparing the two vastly different categories of double dates. When we were with our non-Christian friends, we had a few laughs, but largely we were angry at them. While with them we were uncomfortable, and the next day we would end up feeling guilty and wondering why we thought the non-Christian lifestyle was so much fun. I also wondered why we were so interested in having people like them as friends. But when we were with our Christian friends, we laughed and made jokes in a wholesome environment about things that had nothing to do with sin. And the next day we didn't feel guilty or regretful that we had these people as friends. In fact, we had such a good time with them that I began to ascertain that the Christian life was a much more enjoyable way of life. Shirley and I had specific discussions about this around that time. And our conclusions had a great impact on our becoming Christians. In not so many words, we concluded: inner joy is the source of true fun. Surface jollies are just that: surface. We wanted fun that was clean and deep—not condemning and shallow.

Happiness, inner joy, and peace of mind are companion emotions to laughter and fun. They are inseparable. To say the Christian life offers the greatest sense of inner joy and happiness, and then to prohibit laughter and fun causes great confusion. It rings of contradiction paralleled only by a famous preacher having a prostitute, or a father saying "I love you" to his daughter, and then physically abusing her.

Yes, it is true; the Bible says, "There is...a time to weep and a time to laugh" (Eccl. 3:4). But if—for the church—a time to cry and be serious is most of the time, and the time to laugh and have fun is almost nonexistent, it causes extreme bewilderment in the minds of people trying to find their way to the cross in these days.

No environment is beautiful where laughter is not present. Some men are attractive and some ladies are beautiful whether they are laughing or not. But there is not one person on the planet that doesn't look more beautiful when laughing than when frowning.

Beautiful is the person and the church that laughs.

Chapter 5

⌒

Absence of Expectations

HAVE YOU EVER thought about how hard it is today to become a professional athlete?

Take baseball.

First, you have to be good enough to make the high school team, but not just any high school. It needs to be one with a ranking, because of its size, of AA or higher. Very few athletes are even scouted unless they attend a high school of at least that size.

To make this high school team usually requires years of playing and excelling in little league and the next levels, Babe Ruth Leagues, or whatever they might be called in your area. Then, if you are fortunate enough to have improved your skills to the point where you are the best to go out for the team, you will get the attention of the coaches at high school tryouts. If so, and you perform within the top twenty who try out, you will make the team. If you make this grade, then, during the time you are on the team (two to four years) you need to keep your grades up so you won't have any major participation gaps in your play because of grade ineligibility. And you need to pump weights, work out on your own, come to practice early, and leave late so that you are constantly improving your game. You also need to be fortunate enough to avoid serious injury because colleges are reluctant to sign someone with a history of physical injury.

If you are able to meet these criteria and become the number one or two player on your high school team, that is if your team was good enough to have an excellent record from your influence while you were playing on it, you might attract a level one college's attention and be recruited. Level one is almost a must, because few professional teams ever notice athletes attending lesser schools.

Then, if for a minimum of two years you excel to become the number one or two player on your college team, with all the same disciplines and injury-free blessings you received in high school, you might be drafted by a professional team.

Then, once you have reached this level, in order to actually play and make a living, you need to have the opportunity to showcase your skills to your coaches so they can see that you are among the top players on your pro team. However, to keep playing so that you can be classified as making the pro grade, you will have to continue to excel at the top of your team's players or you will find your stint with the pros very short-lived. In other words, you have to rise to the top and remain at the top of all the top players in the world in order to play at the top level. Piece of cake, right!

That is what it takes to become a professional baseball player these days. There may be a *few* exceptions to these rules, but believe me, there are precious *few*.

The same kinds of tough standards apply to every sport. The trademark of this path is performance. If you perform, you make the grade. If you don't, you're out. Your dreams are dashed, your hopes destroyed, and your unmet goals are a constant reminder of your failure and the haunting fact that you couldn't measure up.

It is not any different in business. The best jobs, making the most money, and gaining the most honor all require peak performance. If you perform, you get promoted. Performance quite often means cheating, lying, or abandoning your family. But that is the price of success. If you don't perform, you don't get the perks. That's all there is to it.

Expectations are high in our world today. And it is that way across the board; in sports, in high school, in business, in clubs, in the job market, in life.

Thomas could never please his father. His dad criticized him for every mistake he made, from the way he ate his food at the dinner table to the way he wrote his name. It drove Paul to drugs.

Richard couldn't please his father either. "Good job, son," never rolled off his father's lips toward his boy. Instead, when Richard would do a task, his father would use words like *idiot, dumb,* or *stupid* to describe his son's performance and his character.

Mary spent most of her life trying to gain the kind of approval her sister received from their mom. But she never could. Even though Mary worked endless hours volunteering in their community and achieving awards and honors her sister never won, still, in their mother's eyes, Mary was lesser.

Nor could Jared find the secret of his dad's validation. Try as he would, he felt he always fell short of the expectations his father had branded somewhere in his mind for his son. No matter what he did, said, or tried, Jared never saw an approving glance or heard a verbal affirmation from his father. And yet, it was all he longed and worked for.

We live in a performance-driven society. In fact, so prevalent is this mindset in our culture, it has distorted our expectations concerning man's potential.

One philosophy concerning man's capabilities says, "Man can do anything." His abilities, his intelligence, his wisdom, his potential, his mind, his power are beyond man's capacity to comprehend. If left to his own devices, mankind has the sufficiency to accomplish anything he sets his mind to.

There are some serious problems with this view.

First, it draws a fine line between performance and arrogance. Humanism is a term that describes an attitude where the ideals and accomplishments of man are central. The end result of this thinking is that humankind is so powerful and capable, who needs God? Man is his own God. The difficulty with this thinking is it walks a tightrope between the ability of man to be all he can be, which is unlimited (says the philosophy), and the kind of pride that goes before a fall. (See Proverbs 16:18.)

The second problem with this view is it doesn't account for the many who diligently ascend the performance mountain, only to fail miserably, falling far short, and giving up along the way. Their falling short is not from their own choice, but by reason of their circumstances—a family crisis, an injury, a moral obligation, a legitimate incompetence. And believe me, there are many such people in sports, in business, and in life. Are they sub-human because they failed? Are they to be deemed less valuable than those who have succeeded and cast aside as unworthy of our time, respect, and praise? Do they get placed on the "Didn't Measure Up" list because they couldn't measure up? Sadly, there are some who feel this is what they deserve.

Nor does this view take into account those who strive to succeed, but fortune's silver-lined cloud darkened for just a moment, and their trek to the top was cut short through no fault of their own.

Sherry was on the road to the top. She had beaten the odds. Her father left home before she ever knew him. Her mother abandoned her. Her grandmother raised her but had no money to send her to college. But nothing was going to stand in Sherry's way. She had the looks. She had the determination. She had the intelligence, the personality, the character, and the grades. She had the stuff. And she told me more than once that she was not going to let her past circumstances get in her way.

But one very average day she drove her car through a green light and was broadsided by a truck driven by a drunk driver. She was in a coma for two months. When she awoke she possessed the mind of a five-year-old, never to grow any older.

Never will she receive accolades for her great accomplishments. Never will she bring credence to the value that performance warrants praise—anyone can do it if they try. Sherry never failed, yet she will never be able to perform to people's standards of success.

She stands as a testimony, along with millions like her, that performance does not equal worth.

Many of the commercials on television, advertisements on billboards, and slogans you see hanging on walls attempt to pound home the idea that man's potential and ability are limitless. Business offices have performance statements hanging all over their walls. Recreational centers post pictures of mountains, rivers, canyons, and wildlife with quips beneath them driving home the power of mankind's strength, will, potential, and ability to persevere. Companies sell products with mottos that depict the themes of performance and high expectations concerning human possibilities, and usually the products are only indirectly related to the slogan. The real selling point is the slogan. Point being, we live in a world that is so impressed with—and so ruled by—the performance and high expectation mentality: if the public identifies with the rationale of the slogan, they will buy the product even if the merchandise is junk. It is akin to "sex sells everything." Only now it is "performance sells everything."

Let me remind you of the problem I presented earlier: people fail. It is a well-known reality. If a club, business, team, enterprise, or society establishes that performance is going to be its battle cry for its constituents, there are going to be a huge percentage of their people broken, bleeding, destroyed, and strewn across the battlefield—because people fail. For every one occupying a corner office, there are fifty who failed to meet the grade.

Can anyone be a Michael Jordan? Can anyone be a Tiger Woods, a Joe Montana, President of the United States, or a corporate CEO? No! Can anyone do his or her best? Yes! And all should try. But the reality is the world is made up of people who for one reason or another fail, and don't do their best, and don't excel, and don't measure up.

The hope and objective of high expectation is high performance. The sad result is we don't value those who fail. Furthermore, those who fail idolize and almost deify those who succeed—to the final destruction of their own self worth. Our society has become one that eulogizes its stars. We worship them, exalt them, adore them, and fantasize about being them. These stars have huge followings of people who almost deify these heroes. And so we see the downside of the performance and high expectation philosophy. Stars who succeed reinforce the failures of those who don't—further diminishing their potential to excel. Hero worship spurs on a few, but it cripples many more than it inspires.

Hero worship always falls short when our key hero is not God.

The beautiful message of the church of Jesus Christ is "we have unlimited worth whether we perform or fail." Our worth is not based on our performance; it is based on God's view of us. This view assesses our worth based upon the unlimited potential there is in God. And in His eyes, regardless of how miserably, how completely, and how often we fail, we are of unlimited worth. In fact, those of us who fail the most, because our failures bring us to a place of brokenness and humility, have the greatest potential as far as God is concerned. It is this way because our state of brokenness will force us to lean on God and draw our power from Him; and with His power spurring us on the universe is the limit.

The messages of the two perspectives are vastly different and in distinct opposition.

TEMPT AND TEST

Having said that, churches and Christians can easily have their value systems so influenced by a performance-driven mentality that "measuring up" is the primary trait they use to gauge the value of people, Christians, church members, seekers, and outright heathens alike. It does not at all make for a beautiful environment. It is rigid, judgmental, harsh, and downright unattractive. It sounds and looks like the Pharisees of Jesus' day and seeks to disqualify people from the faith, if not the environment, rather than attract them to it.

I did a Greek word study on *tempt* and *test*. I learned it was possible for God to test people. He tested Abraham in Genesis 22. He tested His people in the wilderness when He gave them manna to eat. He tested Job. The word test in the Epistle of James is also used to describe some of Satan's allurements of humans. *Test* and *tempt* actually come from the same root word. But this is what I discovered. When Satan tests, he always does so with the express intent to disqualify. He wants to drag those he tempts kicking and screaming into failure. He delights in it. That was his hope with Job and his intent with Jesus.

But when God tests, He is aiming for our success. His intention is to qualify us, and His objective is to pull us up, not down.

Have you ever sensed you were being tested by someone, and you had the strangest sensation that the person's goal was to catch you in a mistake, a fault, or an incompetence of some kind. If you have ever been tested in this way, at the very least, you know the source of the test. But more important, you know there is no more of an unsettling and miserable environment to exist in.

Churches and Christians steeped in a high expectation mentality are more interested in being the spiritual plumb line that others aren't able to come up to, than they are in helping people to make the grade. The expectation is more important than whether or not people can meet it. Consequently, the hope that people make the cut is very much a second priority (if even that). Their first priority is the expectation. If people don't meet it...oh well. In this way,

God's heart to qualify people gives way to Satan's heart to disqualify them.

Ah, but the environment that says "come as you are"—with all your warts, tattoos, shabby dress, crude ways, pierced tongues, colored hair, failed endeavors, sinful pasts, and shattered existences—is beautiful. Jesus said, "Come to Me, all you who labor and are heavy laden" (Matt. 11:28). That is God's heart—and God's plan.

The incredible thing about the environment that says "come as you are" is this. When people feel accepted, they come broken and humble and in deep gratitude for the invitation. (See Luke 14:15–24.) The result is that there are no walls up and no prideful barriers in place to hinder or limit growth and restoration for those who come. They are free to grow in the grace and knowledge of the Lord.

When performance is the criterion, pride becomes the surrounding attitude. People wrap themselves in haughtiness just to safeguard their fragile self-esteem from attack. High expectations have a way of assaulting people and rendering them worthless.

But when acceptance is the prevailing environment, walls come down and barriers are dismantled so that people can change. That is the beauty of "come as you are." First, people feel acceptance. Next, they feel loved and worthy. Third, pride crumbles. And last, new heights, though before not scaleable, can be reached.

Cookie came to our church when she was fifteen years old. Her mother was much more interested in other men than she was in raising her daughter. So for the most part, she abdicated her responsibilities as a mother to her sister, Cookie's aunt. When Cookie came to our church, she was pregnant, shamed by her family, shunned by the teenage boy responsible for her pregnancy, and looking at a lifetime of despair. The walls were way up with Cookie. Yet people saw through her pride, accepted her just the way she was and the walls came down. She found acceptance and God's forgiveness, and she was off and growing.

First, Cookie settled things with her mother, who soon began coming to church. Around the same time, the rest of her family began coming to church as well; her aunt, uncle, and cousins and, like Cookie's mother, they found acceptance and God's forgiveness. Soon our worship leader detected in Cookie a quality singing voice, and she was asked to join a vocal ensemble. Before long she was singing solos and wowing the church with her talent and her heart for God.

At a certain point she caught the eye of our youth pastor. She had a little girl who she was raising by then, but he married Cookie and adopted her daughter as his own. When he left to take his own church, Cookie became a pastor's wife and grew into a capable and honorable leader in their church. Today she and her husband lead a thriving church in Georgia.

Cookie is an example of someone who has performed exceptionally in her life, though all the odds were against her. It wasn't because we draped our church environment in high expectations and performance criteria. I am of the settled opinion that it was because, in her coming, she sensed *no* high expectations that would cause her to feel that she wasn't accepted or didn't measure up. This environment remained constant as she grew in the Lord, and it allowed her to stay broken in humility before God so that His power could have its way in her life. And it allowed her to sense God's smile over her that was the primary catalyst helping to repair, nurture, and develop her into the incredible creature He had always intended her to be. The result: she has exceeded all expectations that anyone may have had for her.

Manuel was selling drugs and drunk most days. His wife and three tiny children came to church and found Christ. They prayed tirelessly for their husband and father. He would show up to church periodically and even come to the altar to receive Christ. Of course when he came, he was fully inebriated. As soon as he was sober, he barely remembered the commitment he had made to God. And it was clear he hadn't meant it. This happened enough times that it caused great discouragement for his family; because instead of his life changing for the better, he would just get into more serious trouble at his job, with his family, and with the law. When he finally gave his life to God sincerely, he was awaiting trial for dealing drugs. No one in our church judged or rejected Manuel for his lifestyle, even when he would come to the altar drunk, because most of the people came from similar backgrounds.

In this environment of acceptance, Manuel thrived. Before long he heard a call from God to ministry. He worked a strenuous job but began to go to Bible college full time while working full time. In three years he graduated with a ministerial diploma.

If a performance criterion had governed the church environment when Manuel began to come, knowing what I knew about him, I am fairly confident he never would have found God, let alone heard a call to ministry. People would have shunned and repelled him long before he ever bowed the knee to Christ. Altar counselors would have stiff-armed him the second they smelled alcohol on his breath at the altar. People would have turned their noses up at him as soon as they learned of his drug dealing. Leaders and church members would have shamed him for his treatment of his wife and kids. And he would have never gotten close to the day when he gave his heart to the Lord.

A beautiful behavior of the church—expressed in a body of believers and in individuals who are part of His church—is one that is absent of expectations for people. Instead the invitation is "come as you are" with all of your junk. The message the church communicates to them about God's love is "God's acceptance and love for you is not—and will never be—based on whether or not you get any better than you are right now. He loves you just as you are."

Chapter 6

∼

A Tale of Two Visions

O NCE UPON A time a young pastor had a vision.
It was an incredible vision. It involved a huge
church filled with people. It would be a multi-faceted
ministry encompassing scores of serving opportunities
for those who became a part. The organization seen in the
vision would become great and influential in the community
it grew up in. Television and radio broadcasts would spread
the news of this dynamic ministry beyond the community
it served. People worldwide would know this ministry was
blessed of God because of its outstanding growth and unique
appeal. This pastor would widen his influence through many
published books and an ever expanding CD and tape distribution. Finances would never be a problem because the
pastor's fame and influence would generate great amounts
of cash flow from the masses, media, and book sales. And
thousands would come to know the Lord through the impact
of this vibrant ministry.

Once upon a time God had a vision. "A great multitude
which no one could number, of all nations, tribes, peoples,

and tongues, standing before the throne and before the Lamb, clothed with white robes, with palm branches in their hands, and crying out with a loud voice, saying, 'Salvation belongs to our God who sits on the throne, and to the Lamb!'" (Rev. 7:9).

Which vision would you like to be a part of?

Some would say they are one and the same vision. But are you able to see the difference? It is true; both may one day have a part in the multitude God saw. But they are vastly different.

In the second vision, God is the object of man's praise.

In the first vision, a church leader is the object of people's—and his own—praise.

Beautiful is the ministry and happy is the participant thereof who has God's vision rather than a man's vision in primary focus.

You have seen how people are used and abused in visions similar to the pastor's, haven't you? It reminds me of Samuel's warning to Israel when they wanted to have a king, so they could be "like all the nations" (1 Sam. 8:5). God told Samuel to "forewarn them, and show them the behavior of the king who will reign over them" (1 Sam. 8:9).

This is what Samuel told the people:

> This will be the behavior of the king who will reign over you: He will take your sons and appoint them for his own chariots and to be his horsemen and some will run before his chariots. He will appoint captains over his thousands and over his fifties, will set some to plow his ground and reap his harvest, and some to make his weapons of war and equipment for his chariots. He will take your daughters to be perfumers, cooks, and bakers. And he will take the best of your fields, your vineyards, and your olive

groves, and give them to his servants. He will take a tenth of your grain and your vintage, and give it to his officers and servants. And he will take your male servants and your female servants and your finest young men and your donkeys, and put them to his work. He will take a tenth of your sheep. And you will be his servants.

—1 Samuel 8:11–17

To clarify, God (through Samuel) told the people that the king would use them, their families, and their possessions to serve his purposes and establish his kingdom.

Lest I communicate the idea that every pastor with a vision uses people in this way, let me say I know of many who don't. But the church leader that is self- and success-centric will do exactly as the king described in 1 Samuel chapter 8. He will endeavor to build his ministry empire at the expense of those who follow him. He will enlist people to run his equipment, build his buildings, play his instruments, sell his recorded sermons, clean his facilities, organize his programs, teach his classes, grow his attendance, further his name, promote his successes, and erect his kingdom.

And my how the people suffer. They are little more than an end to a leader's means. In time they all feel the abuse—not all at once, so the ministry continues without a mass exodus—but they all do feel it.

But there is another side to this coin—God's vision. There is beauty in ministry that is God- and people-centric instead of self- and personal-success-centered. All the outpourings of God's heart and blessing follow the ministries of the leader who is more interested in building Christ's church and not his own, and in promoting God's glory instead of his.

People aren't abused. They aren't oppressed. They sense in their heart of hearts that they are part of God's work and not a human's. The joy they feel as they serve, the value they embrace as they minister, and the purpose they experience as they give of themselves for Christ and His church are apparent.

Ron Mehl was one of the most humble men and pastors I have ever known. Author of several books, he depicts himself as the depraved individual he is in the numerous personal stories he tells about himself. He led one of the largest churches in the United States, having its home in Beaverton, Oregon. But he never talked about his church's size, and especially never attributed any of its growth to himself. Instead, he talked more about how he felt he was the worst pastor that ever led a church.

When church growth investigators and media sources would try to interview him concerning why he felt his church had grown, he would play down his answer and cut the interviews short.

He would say something like, "I can't give you any reasons for why my church has grown. It certainly isn't because of anything our church or I have done right." Then he would give credit to some of the lay people or staff personnel in his church.

Ron Mehl had leukemia. He endured the disease for many years as he continued to pastor. He often shared that periodically he would approach the Lord about why God allowed such a disease to ravage his body, he being a servant of God. But God's decision to not answer with a healing never embittered Pastor Ron. Instead, it made him more humble.

In 2003, Ron Mehl went home to be with the Lord. He continued to preach up until his last few weeks on this earth. Near the end, he couldn't preach standing, so he did so sitting and even laying on a bed. He didn't do this for show. He did it for the reason that to not serve his Lord because he wasn't feeling that strong would have been too self-centered. And he had a few more things he needed to say to his flock before he left them. As he preached in his deteriorating condition, he never complained about his plight. Never did he hint about any acclaim he should receive, either for the growth or size of his church or for his level of dedication. He felt his service to God was the least he could do for all the Lord had done for him.

Some people didn't like Pastor Ron's church because it was too big. Some weren't happy because they didn't receive enough attention from the pastor. But none could say they were abused by Pastor Ron. He was a shepherd who had proper ministry motives well in focus. His church was Christ's church. Its growth was from God's hand, not his own. If anyone tried to transfer glory to him, he straightened them out pronto. His church reflected an environment of beauty.

God helped me to grasp the beauty of this kind of environment. one that shuns the self-centeredness of desiring a big and growing ministry and reaching the masses, but embraces the part of God's heart that genuinely cares for the one. This story is told in detail in my first book, *Touch One*. But for illustration purposes, let me allude to the message of that story.

When I was first converted to Christ, God transformed my heart dramatically. Before my salvation experience, I was very self-centered and sin-focused. After my conversion, pleasing God and caring for people miraculously emerged as a desire in my heart.

When I first came to the Lord, for some reason a dear old man in our church captured my attention. His name was Merle Simpson, but we called him "Brother."

Brother Simpson was an odd old man. He roamed the streets of our small town with a cane and an awkward waddle that received taunts from many of the teenagers that walked or drove by him as he strolled down the sidewalks.

Brother Simpson was quite elderly and had a way of speaking that further caused people to think him a person of peculiarity. At times in church, he would speak up during a testimony portion of a service and begin his discourse speaking normal enough. But each time, like clockwork, a few words into his sharing, his tenderness and nervousness would take over. His words would all slur together and trail off into a high-pitched squeal filled with incoherent sounds and a lot of tears. It was sweet to many of the adults in church, but it further confirmed his oddness to some others, especially the teenagers.

One day Brother Simpson walked into the church and proceeded to ascend the stairs leading up to the vestibule that was adjacent to the back part of the sanctuary of our tiny church. But something happened during his ascent up the stairs to cause him to lose balance and start to fall backwards. He was able to grasp and lean on the railing, but his feeble legs had barely enough strength to keep him from falling. He became stuck in an awkward position and was unable to move. No one came to his rescue because they didn't know what to do. Some were afraid to touch him because they thought him odd.

I was in the vestibule and, hearing the commotion, came to see what the matter was. By the time I arrived at the top of the stairs, Brother Simpson's trepidation and awkward position had caused him to wet himself, further increasing reluctance to help in the minds of those who saw. I ran down the stairs to his rescue, helping him to gain control of his posture, and supported his frame as he hobbled up the stairs. As I was helping him, I looked up in the direction of the vestibule in time to see some of my peers, who had also been attracted to the commotion. They were pointing at me and chuckling because I had to touch Brother Simpson's soiled pants as I helped him.

The whole incident triggered compassion in my heart, and my wife and I began to care for Brother Simpson.

We started to pick him up from his residence to give him a ride to church and then home again after church was over. He lived alone on the second floor of an old boarding house in our small town. And though he wanted to tackle the stairs by himself, we would assist him all the way up the stairs to his door. In time he invited us into his very modest room and that day we were able to learn a little more about this feeble and tender old man.

He had children and had had a wife, but his wife had died and his children had stopped visiting or calling him some twenty years before. As we looked at the pictures on his dresser that had paint peeling badly from each of its surfaces, our hearts broke as we considered the incredible loneliness Brother Simpson must live with every single day.

As we left him that day, my wife and I decided to try to remedy his loneliness—even if just for a little while. We were a few weeks away from December 25, so we decided to give him a Christmas. The last Sunday before the holiday that year when we took Brother Simpson home after church and helped him up the stairs, we brought with us several presents we had purchased for him. We sat on the edge of his bed, adorned with a tattered and stained blanket, and watched as he opened them. After each one he hugged us, cried, and squealed out a gratuitous and heart-wrenching thank you. It was the worst, as we pondered Brother Simpson's plight, and yet by far the best Christmas we have ever experienced.

But somewhere along the line, I lost my way. Right after that (the next January) we went off to Bible college. Upon graduation, God blessed our ministry with growth and many people coming to the Lord. Yet somewhere along my way, my heart for "the one" gave way to the glory of reaching the masses, having a big ministry, and receiving acclaim for it.

It took several years of wayward thinking for me to be ready when God brought an extremely troubled and wayward soul into my life while leading a church in Northridge, California. In a two-and-a-half-year-long counseling experience characterized by ten to twelve pop-in sessions from this strange visitor, God taught me that ministry to the one is much nearer to His heart than ministry to the masses. And He taught me the joy of touching one person redemptively and compassionately is much more glorious than impacting the multitudes. God gave me a glimpse of His heart.

I sat one-on-one over lunch with Pastor Jack Hayford, then pastor of several-thousand member Church on the Way in Van Nuys, California. I had questions I needed to ask him. But at a certain point he seemed to randomly change the subject to a lament he felt he needed to share with me. I wasn't sure what prompted it but I will never forget it.

He said, "Chris, I used to feel I could adequately shepherd every person in my church. And even though it became increasingly harder as the numbers grew, I endeavored to do so because I knew it was pleasing to the Lord. But when the church reached about two thousand people, I just couldn't do it well anymore. It was then that I sorrowfully released the mantle to my staff just to preserve my own sanity, and I endeavored from that point on to put my shepherding energies into touching my leaders. It was a *must* decision, not a *heart* decision."

As Pastor Jack shared this with me, I saw the spirit of a person who, though he led many, had a heart for the one. And if you are ever fortunate enough to meet this great man of God, you will know immediately it is not a perception he tries to convey. It simply flows from his being.

Compare the environment of a church with a vision to reach the masses (whether the church is big or small) and led by a self- and success-centric pastor with the heart of a pastor aimed at the care of one and the glory going straight to God. Both can become large ministries, or both can remain small.

Regardless of size, which environment would you like to exist in?

Part II

∽ *Beautiful, Loving Behaviors* ∾

VOLUMES HAVE BEEN written on the subject of Christian love. It would be impossible for me to write anything new or anything more profound on the subject than what has already been written. So I am not even going to try. What I would like to do is offer you a few fresh perspectives on some old ideas that may help you see more vividly the beauty of Christ's church.

In one of the churches we led as pastors, we began to have gatherings at our home once a month after a morning service for people new to the church. These get-togethers were very informal. They were strictly "get to know one another" meetings: a little food, a little talk, and a lot of laughter.

At one of these events, a young lady in her late twenties by the name of Laura showed up. I remember no details of that gathering, but this is how Laura remembers the day.

To start with, Laura was very uncomfortable because she didn't know what to expect from the Christians who might be at our house. Laura was living with a man outside of marriage and was using pot and cocaine at the time. In short, she was heathen through and through and was ready to defend her heathenism tooth and nail, should anyone challenge her.

But Laura was also very unhappy. That was why she was open to coming to our church when she was invited. And when she heard about the newcomers' meeting, she thought, "Maybe I'll check it out, but my guard is going to be up."

Not long into her time with the people at the gathering, Laura forgot herself and began to have fun. She loosened up and actually started to enjoy the people there. A few times while she was talking with folks, she forgot about the control she was trying to maintain. When she did, she used some profanity and revealed enough of her lifestyle so that people knew she was living with someone outside of marriage. At this realization, she stopped suddenly and looked around. She expected people to put their hands up to their mouths and gasp. But no one did. In fact, it seemed no one was even scathed by her foul language *or* her sin.

She was so shocked that she quit talking and began watching everyone else.

It was an early experience that led to Laura eventually becoming a Christian. As she told me later, she was so surprised that no one rebuked her for her foul language and her sinful lifestyle, she completely changed her opinion about Christians—and therefore God. She concluded: if these Christians accept me the way I am, then God must too.

It was a behavior of the church that was so beautiful, so loving, so authentic, so Christ-like, that it changed a young girl named Laura forever. Genuine, non-judgmental love from members of the church of Jesus Christ. What a novel idea! What a beautiful idea!

In this section you will see six loving behaviors of the church that, I think you will agree, are beautiful. But more importantly, they will help fashion an environment that will better portray the love of God for Christians and unbelievers alike to behold and be attracted to.

Chapter 7

༄

An Atmosphere of Forgiveness

ORGIVENESS, HOW IMPORTANT is that? It's everything," said one pastor.

In Luke chapter 15, Jesus tells three stories one after the other—rapid fire—about how important lost people should be to His followers: a lost sheep, a lost coin, a lost son. This repetitive pattern communicated, at very least, a clear message: lost people are important to God.

In Matthew chapter 18, five pictures are painted—not three but five—by the Master. They are painted, one following the other, all on the subject of forgiveness. All together they let the reader know that forgiveness isn't just another casual subject Jesus was addressing. They shouted: forgiveness is of *paramount* importance to God.

I have included the passages here for your convenient examination. I have identified the five pictures Jesus painted:

1. "Moreover if your brother sins against you, go and tell him his fault between you and him alone. If he

hears you, you have gained your brother. But if he will not hear you, take with you one or two more, that 'by the mouth of two or three witnesses every word may be established.' And if he refuses to hear them, tell it to the church. But if he refuses even to hear the church, let him be to you like a heathen and a tax collector."

—Matthew 18:15–17

2. "Assuredly, I say to you, whatever you bind on earth will be bound in heaven, and whatever you loose on earth will be loosed in heaven."

—Matthew 18:18

3. "Again I say to you that if two of you agree on earth concerning anything that they ask, it will be done for them by My Father in heaven. For where two or three are gathered together in My name, I am there in the midst of them."

—Matthew 18:19–20

4. Then Peter came to Him and said, "Lord, how often shall my brother sin against me, and I forgive him? Up to seven times?" Jesus said to him, "I do not say to you, up to seven times, but up to seventy times seven."

—Matthew 18:21–22

5. "Therefore the kingdom of heaven is like a certain king who wanted to settle accounts with his servants. And when he had begun to settle accounts, one was brought to him who owed him ten thousand talents. But as he was not able to pay, his master commanded that he be sold, with his wife and children and all he had, and that payment be made. The servant therefore fell down before him, saying, 'Master, have patience with me, and I will pay you all.' Then the master of

that servant was moved with compassion, released him, and forgave him the debt. But that servant went out and found one of his fellow servants who owed him a hundred denarii; and he laid hands on him and took him by the throat, saying, 'Pay me what you owe!' So his fellow servant fell down at his feet and begged him, saying, 'Have patience with me, and I will pay you all.' And he would not, but went and threw him into prison till he should pay the debt. So when his fellow servants saw what had been done, they were very grieved, and came and told their master all that had been done. Then his master, after he had called him, said to him, 'You wicked servant! I forgave you all that debt because you begged me. Should you not also have had compassion on your fellow servant, just as I had pity on you?' And his master was angry, and delivered him to the torturers until he should pay all that was due him. So My heavenly Father will also do to you if each of you, from his heart, does not forgive his brother his trespasses."

—Matthew 18:23–35

Especially important to Jesus, it seems, is the atmosphere of forgiveness in the church. It is interesting that this is the second and only mention that Jesus makes referencing the church—the other one being where He said, "I will build My church" (Matt. 16:18). Here in Matthew 18 He is talking about how to keep its atmosphere functional and healthy.

I don't want to sermonize here. But let me briefly itemize just a few of the powerful points Jesus makes in this passage about forgiveness.

1. In verse 15, Jesus says the motive of forgiveness is to "gain" your brother—or sister, aunt, niece,

nephew, uncle, cousin, or just another Harry in the church. Jesus wants a church filled with healed and "gained" relationships; not sick, clashing, and divided ones.

2. In verse 16, He says to use witnesses to help bring people back together in unity so that others take part in the process of forgiveness and to further insure reconciliation through relationships that are accountable.

3. In verse 17, He tells the church if the bitter party refuses to forgive, it should make a final determination that the man is a heathen and expel him from the number of those who believe. I think there are two obvious reasons for this. First, the man's expulsion was to cleanse the church environment of the spirit of unforgiveness. And second, to let the whole church know that there is no place in the beauty of His church for the ugliness of unforgiveness.

4. In verse 18, Jesus talks about the negative power of unforgiveness to bring spiritual bondage into the church environment. Forgiveness will do the opposite. It will actually loose and release spiritual bondage from the overall atmosphere of the church.

5. In verse 19, Jesus tells us that forgiveness enables believers to come together in love and power so that prayers can be answered, so that needs can

be met, and so that they can see God's hand at work in their lives.

6. In verse 22, Jesus tells us that no offence against us is great enough to place a limit on the amount of times we should forgive someone.

7. And beginning in verse 23 in His masterpiece parable on forgiveness, Jesus shows us that forgiving offences against us from people is our reasonable service considering the enormous debt of sin God has forgiven us.

I suppose we could identify many more points about forgiveness in these five snapshots on the matter. The passage is bulging with truths on the subject. And it all illustrates the fact that forgiveness between people is vitally important to God. It also tells us He is adamant about an air of forgiveness being present in His church and in the heart of His followers.

But let me make it very clear. An atmosphere of forgiveness in the church begins with leadership. Leadership needs to pioneer and model it in order to pave the way for a cleansed environment of forgiveness.

In my first church, God was teaching me how to lead people. I was just a kid in my mid to late twenties. Looking toward one Sunday, I decided to teach on forgiveness. I had spent the entire week preparing my sermon, and on Saturday afternoon, I was putting some final touches on my presentation when God spoke to me. Just as clear as when my wife would reprimand me for not cleaning up a mess, I heard God say, "You can't preach this sermon until you get it right with Joe—until you clean up this little mess in your life."

Joe M. was the pastor of the last church I worked at as youth pastor just before I came to the church I was leading at that time. I had been there for only a year, but when I left Joe's church, my leaving wasn't the best. In departing I had become the pastor of a church about an hour's drive time away and occasion hadn't brought us together since, so the issues were easy to leave undisturbed. I knew I had unforgiveness issues with Joe, but I preferred to ignore them. And their buried place in my heart kept them neatly tucked away from the forefront of my consciousness.

However, that Saturday afternoon God was *not* ignoring them, and He wasn't going to allow me to ignore them any longer either.

I suspected Joe might not be free on that short notice, and he wasn't. But when I called him that day, I set up a lunch with him and our wives for the following Monday. In keeping with the reprimand I had sensed from the Lord, I told my church on Sunday about God's word to me, the details of the issue between myself and Joe, and about the lunch I had scheduled for the next day. I felt peace that this would satisfy the heart of God.

At the lunch I apologized to my former pastor and boss for my foolishness and begged his forgiveness, which he granted.

The service in between that Saturday and Monday wasn't particularly powerful. My sermon hadn't been that effective, apparently. I remember feeling, "I must have bombed. The people weren't that responsive. I hope they got the message."

But the church of Jesus Christ is much more than a Sunday morning service. And over time, it seemed that the people had had stamped on their hearts that day a powerful message just the same—more from my confession than my sermon. It was a message proclaiming how important forgiveness is to God.

And I came to understand—God had set me up. The timing of His word to me being Saturday—not earlier in the week—forced me to have to tell my church about the issue in order to be obedient to His impression on me: to confess before I preached my sermon. In telling the church on that Sunday, though I didn't consciously do it for this reason, I was modeling forgiveness. At that time in my life and ministry, I wouldn't have willingly confessed such an embarrassing failure to my church. But God is not averse to doing a little arm-twisting to get his stubborn and clueless servants to do what He needs them to do.

Around that time, a rash of unforgiveness issues began to resolve themselves both between people and between people and God. And our church saw a surge of growth. For some time I thought it was because God had blessed my obedience, and I patted myself on the back for being so in touch with God (oh, what a soiled heart!). But later I realized it was nothing of the kind. Instead, I knew, it was an environment transformation. The beauty of a church filled with hearts cleansed of unforgiveness became visible, and people had become drawn to it.

Forgiveness is an arm of love, but it is a big arm. When Jesus said in John 13:35 to love one another that all men might know that you are my disciples, He was also saying forgiveness will have to be a constant in order to continue to make this verse true.

I have also found that forgiveness is a maintenance issue. Like every other spiritual quality, if left unattended, the conviction to seek forgiveness will in time fade from the hearts of men and women. Don't expect unforgiveness to be thwarted one time and you will never have a problem with it again. Unforgiveness will infect and contaminate the love environment in a church and there need to be, if not structured systems, at very least, patterns of elimination being presented to the church. I am referring to patterns like modeling by leadership, teaching on the subject, direct but loving confrontation, testimonies about forgiveness, and prayer for people struggling with the issue.

At one point we had two college girls who roomed together teaching our children's ministry during our Sunday morning service. They were friends, but their constant exposure to each other at home, at school, in daily activities, and at church was beginning to grate on the two of them. They were getting on each other's nerves wherever they went, including church. One of the other teachers informed me of their ongoing feud and that the kids had to witness the war going on between the two girls every time they taught.

"Debbie, would you get that pencil for me?"

"Get it yourself, Charla. I'm not your slave."

"Why do you have to act so snippy?"

"Me? You're the one who is aggravating."

Right in front of the kids! The children were turning their heads back and forth, as if they were observing a tennis match, with their mouths open in awe watching the drama between the two girls. One would serve up an insult, and the other one would return it.

I called the two young college girls into my office the next Sunday after church. This is what I said to them.

"It has come to my attention that you aren't getting along very well."

They looked at each other with daggers in their eyes and conceded that indeed there was a problem.

"But Debbie's such a jerk all the time."

"Yeah, but you're the annoying one."

I quickly stopped them before they killed each other right there in front of me and I said, "Girls, first of all, this is not pleasing to God. He wants you loving one another, not hating one another. I know you are probably starting to get a little sick of each other, but your fighting is starting to affect our church and your ministry to our kids. People are noticing, and it says to me it is starting to get out of hand."

They hung their heads in shame, but the daggers were still in their eyes.

I said, "This is what we are going to do. Debbie, you and Charla are going to stay here in my office until you love each other. I don't want the two of you to go home until this situation between you is resolved and each of you has completely forgiven the other. When you love each other again, come to my house and let me know. There are only two rules: no hitting and no throwing things."

I lived close to the church, and they both knew where that was. I bid them farewell and left them to their own devices. I was a little apprehensive because I didn't want a murder to take place on the church property—especially in my office. But I left them there just the same.

About an hour later there was a knock on my door, but it wasn't from the two girls. One of our board members had come to the church to do something, and he heard the two going at each other in my office. He wanted to make sure I knew about it.

He said, "Pastor, did you know that there are two girls in your office, and they are about to kill each other? Do you think I should stop it?"

I smiled, though a bit nervously, and said, "No, I am going to trust that they are going to be able to work it out on their own."

Two and a half hours later there was another knock on my door. This time it was Charla and Debbie. They had big smiles on their faces and their arms were around each other.

"Pastor," Debbie said, "Thank you for treating us with tough love. It was the best lesson we have ever been taught."

I told them that I was proud of them and had every confidence they would come away from their meeting loving each other.

I hugged them, prayed with them, closed the door, turned to my wife, and said, "Thank God that is over with. We won't have to call the coroner after all."

A Cleansing

Because we are human, we are all prone to allowing issues of anger and unforgiveness to rise up in our lives and gatherings. Left unattended, those issues can create a "spirit of schism" between people and ultimately the church. If that happens, the environment of love that is so crucial for effective nurturing and community development can become buried under an ever-growing layer of coldness and resentment. You can feel it between people, and it will seriously hinder the church's ministry.

In one church we went to as pastors, we experienced resistance from the start. It seemed the more we tried to love people, the more they resisted our love and us. It was a frustrating and confusing time in our ministry.

The church housed a Christian school that had its beginnings in the church. When I arrived, the school was not doing well at all. Attendance was down. Finances were low.

And the school was taking a severe toll on both the morale and the facilities of the church.

Furthermore, the school board had discovered that the school's principal had done some questionable things with the institution's finances. When they approached the principal, he reacted defensively and shamed them for suggesting that he would do something so despicable. They tried to approach him about it a few more times and each time he responded poorly. So in anger at him, they reported it to the authorities. Mind you, the board members all had children in the school, and their resentment was linked to the fact that they had entrusted their children to the integrity they were expecting from the principal. In their view, he had not only violated their trust, he had demonstrated to their children a poor example of Christianity.

When I came on the scene as pastor, the principal hated the board, and the board hated the principal. And I was the one inheriting the task of trying to resolve the problem.

To make a long story short, the school moved out of our church and tried to make it in another facility but dissolved rather quickly. The principal was arrested and convicted on criminal charges having to do with how he handled the school's money. He served less than a month in jail, but the state took his teaching credentials away from him, never allowing him to teach in a school again. He still attended and remained connected to our church throughout the time of the school's leaving and eventual closing, and throughout the time of his trial and imprisonment.

At one point in the middle of the ordeal, I recall meeting with the board of the school and begging them, for the sake of being forgiving and obedient to the scripture in 1 Corinthians 6:1–11, to try to handle the situation within the Christian community rather than going to the authorities. But the resentment was impenetrable. They wouldn't hear of it. They weren't the least bit moved by the scripture's exhortation.

But be assured, the principal was bitter too.

Yet, it seemed to be behind all of us and our church when the school dissolved and was no longer connected to our fellowship.

Around this time, as in my first church, I decided (more randomly than deliberately) to speak one Sunday morning on the subject of forgiveness. God had done a tremendous thing in my life concerning my relationship with one of my brothers. The details of the reconciliation between us were miraculous and life-changing. Though my spiritual sensors weren't necessarily in tune with the unforgiveness issues in my church, apparently God's omniscience sensors were. And He prompted me to share my story in a Sunday morning service.

At the conclusion of the service, I stressed the importance God places on forgiveness between people. Then I encouraged folks that if there was any unforgiveness in their hearts for someone else, to go and make it right as soon as possible.

After the service, I was surprised, yet pleased, to see several people in small groups in tucked away corners of the church talking privately.

One couple in particular had pulled the principal and his wife aside and was talking quietly to them. This couple had shown a fair amount of resistance to us when we arrived on the scene as pastors, and were a part of the resistance I referred to earlier. The next week this couple came to me and told me the details of their meeting with the principal and his wife.

It seems that this couple once had their children enrolled in the school. However, at a certain point, though they had helped the school to get its start, they began to see its attendance and appearance going downhill and perceived the quality of the learning environment to be diminishing. So, a little miffed at the principal for what they believed to be his less than adequate leadership, they decided to pull their kids out of the school. Then, when they saw the charges against the principal being publicized in the newspaper, it fanned the flames of their resentment even more.

When they heard my story on forgiveness, they were prodded by the Holy Spirit that they had allowed bitterness to settle into their hearts. So they went directly to the principal and his wife seeking reconciliation. What they didn't know was that the principal had been harboring some pretty serious resentment in his own heart toward this couple.

These two couples had been close friends. Along with others in the church some years before, they had the vision to start the school. So as a team, together they launched the dream. But as time wore on and this couple's trust for the principal's leadership diminished, they drew away from them. Then, they withdrew their kids from the institution when the school was struggling financially and with a morale deficit, without an explanation. The principal began to feel deep feelings of resentment for them. None of this was ever discerned or dealt with.

Each Sunday these couples would come to church resenting each other, never talking to the other outside of small talk, and, in effect, allowing the bitterness in each of their hearts to go unchecked and to fester.

I am happy to say they resolved their unforgiveness that Sunday morning. But it all taught me a valuable lesson.

The slightest bit of resentment can allow a kind of relational poison to seep into the church. But that can lead to greater amounts of the same poison being released into the fellowship. When one person harbors resentment, that resentment has a way of condoning it in another, and then another. And if it goes unchecked, even more will become exposed to the poison. Once it gets loose, it can trigger a rash of criticism, anger, discord, and bitterness in an entire body. When that happens, all is just about lost because all manner of divisiveness and quenching of the Holy Spirit can be unleashed.

When immorality threatened the church at Corinth, Paul advised in his first letter to the church to excommunicate the offender (or at least treat him as if he were a heathen) because only a heathen could do what he had done. (See 1 Corinthians 5:1–8.) Then in his second letter to the church, Paul advises, "You ought rather to forgive and comfort him, lest perhaps such a one be swallowed up with too much sorrow" (2 Cor. 2:7). Then he says, "Now whom you forgive anything, I also forgive. For if indeed I have forgiven anything, I have forgiven that one for your sakes in the presence of Christ, lest Satan should take advantage of us; for we are not ignorant of his devices" (2 Cor. 2:10–11).

There, did you catch it? Paul is stating the absence of forgiveness, regardless of what someone has done, is a device of Satan—one with which he can infect the church. Earlier Paul didn't want the spiritual disease of immorality to infect the Corinthian church. But at a certain point he recognized the spiritual disease of unforgiveness could become Satan's contaminating agent.

The church is truly beautiful when it is filled with Christ's love and maintains that love environment by keeping immediate and full forgiveness on the front burner of its awareness.

It would be foolish to assume that a Christian should never have a problem with another person; that they should always love other people with no ripples in their relational waters. Our sinful nature resists that prospect with successful regularity. It is much wiser to assume that everyone will have a problem with someone else at some point—and probably at several points. And since this is true, an environment of resolution needs to be created, cultivated, and maintained. That way people won't deny the obvious, and they will have permission and a model to seek resolution and forgiveness rather than allow their resent ment to fester and contaminate the church.

The most beautiful behavior of the church I know of is love. Love can never continue to exist in a church or in a person unless forgiveness is at that person's or that churches' beck and call.

Chapter 8

~

The Good Side of
Spiritual Blindness

JESUS MADE IT clear: to be spiritually blind is bad. Very
bad! People who are spiritually blind think the preaching
of the cross—even the concept of the cross—is foolishness. (See 1 Corinthians 1:18.) The spiritually blind aren't
able to see or understand the meaning of the deep things of
God. (See 1 Corinthians 2:9–10.) Those who can't see spiritually aren't able to comprehend spiritual truth and are clueless
as to the meaning of many (if not all) of the parables Jesus
told. (See Matthew 13:13–16.) So, spiritual blindness is not a
good thing.

But Peter tells us about a kind of spiritual blindness that
is good and, it seems, very pleasing to God. It is the kind
of spiritual blindness that is able to look past sinfulness
and failure and mistakes. The reason it is good is because
its source is love. "And above all things have fervent love
for one another, for love will cover a multitude of sins"
(1 Pet. 4:8). Proverbs agrees, "Hatred stirs up strife, but
love covers all sins" (Prov. 10:12).

Most of us are familiar with this basic concept. All of us have people we love. And it is much harder to be objective concerning those people than it is a perfect stranger. We see the flaws of people unfamiliar to us long before we do those we love.

To clarify, I am not talking about blind denial.

I know a lady who thinks the sun rises and sets on her daughter Melody (not her real name). And my does she love her daughter. She thinks Melody to be the purest, sweetest, kindest, most wholesome girl in the town in which they live. From the view of Mom, Melody can do no wrong. But from the view of others, Mom is as blind as a bat. Melody is moody, mean, selfish, and not nearly as pristine as her mother thinks her to be.

I also know of a man who thinks the same way about his son Micky (not his real name). His father loves his son so much and to him Micky is the ideal boy, the best Christian, and the finest example of honor and sobriety he knows. Little is his dad aware that Micky cusses like a sailor, engages freely in sexual transgressions with his girlfriend, and is quite the lush when he is out with his college buddies.

"Could this be a good kind of spiritual blindness," you ask? No, not when it slips into the denial we see in these examples. But the kind of love that looks past sin, questionable behavior, failures, cocky attitudes, rebellious tendencies, and carnal actions to see the potential child of God inside a person is the most glorious and God-like kind of blindness in existence.

God does not overlook sin. He is not blind to our iniquities. He sees them and does not condone them. But once forgiven, He forgets them (see Isaiah 43:25) and separates us from them. (See Psalm 103:12.) But nowhere in the Bible does it say He doesn't see them. Yet God is able to look past our sin with His love. It is the character of His grace. And it is the power of His Son's spilt blood. His love—affirmed by Jesus' shed blood—enables God to look past our sin. It is the kind of blindness God has and desires us to have when we encounter sin.

In Jesus' day, those who resisted Christ saw all the outward signs of sin in people. They were the religious leaders. And these so-called religious leaders judged these sinners to be untouchable, unredeemable, disgusting representatives of the society of the forever lost.

In Matthew chapter 23 Jesus paints some ugly pictures of the spirituality of these self-named Godly people. He says (my paraphrase):

> Do what they say, not what they do (v. 3). They do their good deeds not to be seen by God, but by men (v. 5). They are interested in their own glory not God's (vv. 6–13). They criticize people committing the slightest sins while they commit the worst sins themselves (v. 24). They clean up their outward appearance to be thought holy, but inside themselves, they are spiritually filthy (v. 27). They honor the Godly who have been martyred for the Lord's work by decorating their tombs; when in fact, these men would be their murderers if given the opportunity (vv. 30–31).

Wow! Don't be a scribe or Pharisee.

It has always been a marvel to me how certain people in churches are able to see the flaws in the spiritually deficient, while others seem to be blind to their shortcomings.

When Penny (not her real name) first came to our church, she was impenetrable. She was as hard as a rock and twice as cold. Every time she attended she dressed in black or dark gray and wore clothing that looked more like something a man would wear than a woman. Her hair was groomed and shaped into a style that looked way more masculine than feminine.

The second time Penny visited, our church was holding a "get to know the pastor" gathering for visitors at our home. Sensing her pain, someone in our church pigeon-holed her into coming. From there, we loved her into our fellowship.

In time Penny's story came to light. Her father, a part-time minister, had molested her almost every night for seven years when she was a little girl, while her mother, a nurse, worked the night shift. As a result she grew to be an adult with a repulsion for men. She wanted to look like a man so men wouldn't be attracted to her. For a short time during her twenties, Penny experimented with a lesbian lifestyle, but the biblical foundation in her life would not permit her to pursue it for very long. She let it go and in time decided to try to find a church where she could rekindle her relationship with God.

After she had been coming to our church for about a year, we were able to win her trust enough for her to feel she could share this information with us. However, it took longer for her style of grooming to change.

The next fall several of our ladies, including Penny, attended a women's conference in the Southern California area. My wife, Shirley, was one of the leaders at that conference. At one point, someone came to her with several ladies and told her they had discerned there was a woman at the conference that was a lesbian and was there to prey sexually on the women attending. Though there were hundreds of women there, my wife knew instantly they were referring to Penny. She quizzed them to be certain, and when she was,

Shirley told them Penny came to our church and that they were in no danger. Then she gently scolded them for jumping to conclusions before she sent them on their way.

Honestly, this group of ladies had seen some things accurately. They had just not seen them through the lens of love. If they had, they would have been able to look past the outward appearances of a troubled and vulnerable life to see the heart of someone in the process of God's transformation. How beautiful are the blind eyes of those filled with God's love.

In the first two years after the year 2000, a clothing style emerged among teenage girls that included hip-hugging jeans, or pants with a top that was tight to the body but did not cover the tummy completely. A new family came to our church around that time, and both the father and his teenage daughter had incredible singing voices. So our worship leader moved them quickly onto the worship team, where our church could benefit from their talent, and where they could flourish in the use of their gifts. But the daughter, being a teenager, was into this clothing style—as was most every other girl in our church. She wore modest tops revealing an inch or less of her abdomen between her pants and top. I saw it and assessed in my mind, "It's fine. Besides, she dresses neatly."

But after this young girl had sung a few times, a man in our church came to me and voiced his disapproval. He was convinced he had detected a transgression worthy of protest and wanted the frivolous display of flesh stopped at once. I took it under advisement and talked to our church leadership about it. United, they felt with me that what she was wearing was fine, especially given the fact that we wanted to have a church that was culturally sensitive and open to people wearing all manner of unusual attire. The style wasn't unusual, but it was relevant.

The next time she was on the worship team and wore the same style of clothes, this man was in my face again. This time he demanded that I do something about it. I calmly explained to him that I had taken his previous observation to church leadership and we decided—given the vision of our church to reach out and that her usage of the style was modest—that we would allow her to continue to dress that way while singing on the worship team. He stormed away, angry that we had not heeded his suggestion.

A few weeks later another lady approached me about the same thing. And after I had said to her what I said to the other critical man, she too stomped off in a huff. It grieved me and reminded me of the way the religious leaders of Jesus' day were so observant of the sins in people, while it seemed as if Jesus hardly even noticed. Or at very least, He made it a point to look past their sin in order to draw them in.

And I thought, "My how people need for the church to look past people's hard and sinful exteriors—the tattoos, the spiked hair, the nose rings, the colored hair, the butt-hanging jeans, and even a little bit of skin. Those things are just smoke screens covering the vulnerable lives inside that need a savior. If we don't look past those things, how will they ever know we love them? How will they ever know God loves them?"

From a different church, Rebecca had finally persuaded her husband to come. His primary contention had been—he had *no* good clothes to wear. He was a former gang member, so his clothing style leaned more in the direction of a gang-banger. She had convinced him that our church was different—that everyone comes to church the way they are. So he agreed to come. However, when they pulled into the parking lot, the first few people he saw wore a shirt and tie. And he refused to come in. He told his wife she could go, but he would wait in the car.

When she came in the front door of the church, she looked downcast. The head usher, who was the only person in the church Rebecca's husband knew, happened to be dressed in a full suit that day. He had just bought it and was showing it off. He noticed she seemed discouraged and asked her what was wrong. After she told him, he went into the restroom and took his suit jacket, vest, shirt, and tie off. All that was left was a wife-beater (a flimsy tank top) for an undershirt that he left on and hanging over his pants, and his shoes. Then he went to the car where Rebecca's husband was sitting. In a few minutes they both came through the front doors with smiles on their faces. That day the head usher collected the offering wearing a flimsy wife-beater undershirt with upper arm tattoos and a hairy back on display for all to see. And Rebecca's husband gave his heart to the Lord.

Diane (not her real name), her husband, and their two children came to church one Sunday. Word travels fast in the Christian community, even in the city, and Diane's story preceded her.

Diane was the pastor's secretary in the last church her family attended. But something happened. Her relationship with her husband had been waning for some time. Her pastor's kind words and gentle ways had been working on her for months and suddenly the unthinkable happened, an affair with Pastor Dan (not his real name).

It only lasted a few weeks. It was discovered by a church member who happened to see them rendezvous at a hotel in a nearby community. And just like that, her family, Pastor Dan's family, and their church all went into tailspins that landed each of the entities in their own private wrecks on the side of sin's road.

Everyone heard about it. It was the talk of the church community for a month.

Pastor Dan's wife left him and took their four children with her. In shame he left the area and went to his home in a nearby state to seek support from his family.

The church almost didn't survive. People didn't want to be associated with a church possessing that kind of reputation. So they left in droves. And those still attending wanted nothing to do with Diane. She was the home-wrecker splitting up the pastor's family; and she was the church wrecker. Within a month of the discovery, the vibrations the church members sent her drove her—along with her family—out the church doors.

Diane's husband, Jim (not his real name), was broken and her family was hurting as well. But he was a tender man and was willing to forgive his wife and accept her back if she would go with him to counseling. For six months Diane and her family stayed out of church completely.

Then one Sunday they walked through the front doors. One lady who knew her walked over to Diane and embraced her. The lady's husband shook Jim's hand and welcomed him. Another couple moved toward Jim and Diane to welcome and comfort them.

The rest is history. Diane and Jim had a new church home.

They sought God's forgiveness and spent much time praying at the altars because their new church home provided a safe place for them to be broken before the Lord, and healed. None of the acceptance from their new church communicated to them that the church was condoning Diane's sin. Jim and Diane knew what she did was wrong. And they felt much shame for all the pain they had gone through and caused. They just needed for someone to love and accept them anyway. They needed someone to look past their sin.

We all know they wouldn't have received a reception like that in many churches, Christian groups, or with many Christians. What is the ingredient that made the difference in this particular church?

I call it the good side of spiritual blindness. Genuine believers whose relationship with God was alive and vital were sensitive enough to the heart of Christ to look past their sin and failure as Christ would, to see the vulnerability and needy heart within. They really didn't see or care about any sin that might be present.

I have a friend named Bobby who went to an area in Colorado to start a church. He didn't bring a team with him to help him; nor did he have a lot of money. The only thing he could think to do was start going to the local county jail to minister to the inmates. His thought was, "Most of these people don't have anyone to love them or help them once they are released. Maybe they will come to church."

They did.

As people came to his church, Bobby trained them to not look at the sultry appearances of others. He taught his people to look past their crude mannerisms and to be blind to their past sins. He instructed his church to accept them as Jesus accepted Matthew and Zacchaeus who were considered by the Pharisees to be sinners, tax collectors, traitors, and outcasts of Israel.

Today Bobby has a strong church. About half of its members are ex-cons who have been transformed by the blood of Jesus and the love of His church. Recently Pastor

Bobby left that church to take another. But he left it in the hands of Pastor Dave, who has the same heart as Bobby.

Of all the beauty that exists in Christ's church, I don't think I have ever seen anything more attractive, more glorious, and more reflective of the radiance of God's love than this kind of spiritual blindness.

Chapter 9

~

To Soar...Restore

A FEARED AND MISUNDERSTOOD scripture is
1 Timothy 5:20. This is what it says: "Those who
are sinning rebuke in the presence of all, that the
rest also may fear."

It is feared because people are naturally terrified of
confrontation of any kind. Don't stir up the waters, let
sleeping dogs lie, people say. If you just let the thing be, then
no one will be uncomfortable. Tangible peace for the present
is always preferred over possible peace for the long haul. No
one considers that confrontation concerning misconduct or
sin is not only the most loving thing to do, it is the most
biblical and caring thing to do when a brother or sister in
Christ is caught in a sin.

This scripture is misunderstood because of its criteria: sin.
No one wants to call sin, sin, even in the church. If we identify
what Suzie did as sin, it might embarrass her. If we call what
Jimmy did iniquity, then it will bring condemnation down
on everyone else doing something similar. Or if we rebuke
sin, the world will think us Christians to be judgmental and

cruel, or people will know the ugly truth—we aren't perfect. Or it might cause an eruption in our church, the likes of which we've never seen before.

It is a verse people just don't know how to treat.

Granted, there have been abuses of this kind of confrontation over the years. People have spoken the truth about someone's sin, but not in love. (See Ephesians 4:15.) And people have compelled others to confess their faults, but not so they could be healed. (See James 5:16.) And believers have addressed anger, bitterness, and unforgiveness in others, but not so they could win or gain their brother or sister in Christ. (See Matthew 18:15.) Consequently the flesh has poisoned an effective and biblical method of cleansing, loving, and restoring.

It should never be thought that confrontation must always have an immediate happy ending, or that it was wrong to do it, because the attitude of the person being confronted is sometimes entwined in their sin and may be at the source of the problem. In fact, a negative reaction may be a confirmation that there was indeed sin in that person's life that needed to be addressed. In addition, a negative reaction doesn't necessarily mean the message didn't get through, that the confrontation was done wrongly, or that it should never have been done in the first place.

When I was ten years old, my parents allowed me to get the pet of my dreams—a collie just like Lassie. It was the best dog, and I named him Chum after another collie puppy our family had a few years before, which had died of distemper.

Chum was beautiful, smart, and loving and went with me everywhere. One day when Chum was about eight months old and was walking with me down the sidewalk, he crossed the road in front of a car. I screamed, "NO CHUM!" But it was too late. The car hit my dog with a thud, and I watched as my best friend rolled over and over beneath the car as the vehicle eventually came to a stop. Chum lay on the road breathing hard and whimpering in pain. His beautiful golden-blonde and white fur was shining and matted with his blood. His head was twisted back over his shoulder rocking back and forth while he looked at me, as if he were beckoning for my help.

I rushed to Chum's side as the *murderer* got out of her car and moved toward my dog and I in the middle of the street. Chum was in obvious pain and in desperate need of love and comfort, which I was prepared to give in spite of how bloody it would make me. But when I reached down to touch him, he snarled his teeth and snapped at me as if I were a perfect stranger. How could I know at ten years old and with my dog's limited understanding that at that moment he thought me to be a threat? Later my mother helped me to see that Chum didn't understand either my intentions or the situation. He was in desperate pain, in a fight for his life, and instinctively thought I was part of the problem.

That happens in confrontation sometimes. Even when a rebuke is done in love, its accuracy will touch a nerve in the one being confronted; and that person will react to the pain, blaming the individual who is actually trying to help. And it is because they don't really understand the situation. The pain they feel interprets the confrontation as being done to hurt them. But confrontation of sinful behavior should not be avoided because we are afraid of a misunderstanding any more than I shouldn't have tried to comfort Chum because he might not understand and snap at me.

So many loving and sin-altering confrontations that needed to take place didn't, because people were afraid of the snap, the snarl, and the misunderstanding.

I, too, am not fond of confrontation. I don't like the discomfort that is involved. Nor do I enjoy the momentary disruption of peace. And I know the risk involved. I know the whole thing may blow up in my face. I may lose relationship, trust, or both with the one I am approaching, and it may be for life. It is a huge risk. So I prefer not to confront. But there have been a few times in my ministry when I knew I must to obey scripture, to head off a disaster, and to help exact healing and growth in the person needing to be approached. And sometimes, the overall environment of love or holiness in our church demanded it.

This first example is a snapshot of my dog's accident.

There was a man in one of the churches I led as pastor who was a very talented musician. He could do things with the guitar that most guitarists would not think possible. But this man was also as angry a person as I had ever met. His father had physically and emotionally abused him his entire childhood and did not discontinue when his son moved into adulthood. He continued to mete out mental abuse to his boy through phone calls, visits, and holiday homecomings.

This man, actually in his thirties when he came into my life, was so filled with anger, he constantly spewed it out toward anyone who challenged him. And he had done so throughout his life. In college he was confronted by the dean for insubordinate behavior and finally expelled, so he held a grudge and hated the dean.

The experience formed mistrust in his heart for all authority, including spiritual authority. Then, when he would go to a church and his anger would flare up (which was inevitable because the issues were within *him*, not with leadership), naturally he would be challenged. This further confirmed in his mind that he was justified in hating all church leadership.

But in time, Christians in general were also on his hate list.

Then there was God. Naturally he also had deep angry and hateful feelings toward God, because, ultimately, all of the rejection he felt came from church leadership and Christians, who were God's people. So he blamed their God for the way they reacted to him.

Needless to say, this man was an angry mess. And many would wonder how someone who felt this way about Christians, ministers, and God could even be a Christian. I'll let God be the judge of that.

I saw his heart because he shared it with me often, and I had great compassion for his pain. I told him, because of the anger in his heart and the difficult time he had working with Christians, it would not be healthy for him to work directly with our worship team. Since the team was made up of Christians and he had an underlying detestation for them, it would inevitably antagonize the bitterness he felt even more; and he needed time to be healed. He understood and agreed to sit out and just receive.

But he would constantly hint to some day being able to play on the worship team. I watched him mellow outwardly in his attitude over a two-year period and listened to his hints. Finally I felt he may be ready to play. However, there were a few issues that concerned me, and I felt I needed to talk with him about them first. If he was able to own these issues, he would be ready to play. To be sure I was correct concerning the issues, I ran them by someone in the music ministry and a few people in leadership who knew him well. They agreed they were valid things to address with him before he would minister on our worship team.

So I set a date and proceeded to lovingly and gently talk to him about the issues.

His reaction: snap, snarl, and complete misunderstanding.

It brought me immediately back to the day I leaned over Chum's blood-matted and broken body. Just as Chum didn't understand and snapped at his master, this man interpreted my gentle desire to help as another act of aggression toward him. All the other church leaders and Christians in his life had run him over, and now I was out to hurt him as well. He didn't understand I was trying to help him. He left our church in a huff and viciously slandered my reputation with whoever would listen. He was still snarling.

Am I sorry I confronted him? At first I have to admit, I questioned myself about it. But as I examined my heart, the truly kind way I had approached him, and the confirmations I had received from people, I concluded I had done the right thing.

Here is what the confrontation did. It brought this man back to a fork in his life—one he had stood in front of many times. He was also at this fork every time a situation, authority, or a challenge was presented to him to either trust or blame a leader. At this fork he had the opportunity to choose one of two roads: one that would lead toward healing, growth, humility, maturity, and wholeness; and one leading to the muck and mire of foolishness. Unfortunately, as in each of the other challenges in his life, he chose the lesser road.

Confrontation brings the one being confronted to this fork. It's a chance for a new beginning for that person. If they are stuck somewhere down the lesser road, it is very difficult for them to find their way back to the fork on their own. Loving confrontation by addressing their sin or failure speeds them back to the fork where a new start can take place.

But in a church, it also does something else. It cleanses a church body of a cancer of sin that can have destructive effects on the overall climate of a fellowship. And if the person takes the *high* road, it can bring a spark of new life to a gathering of believers.

In the first church I led as pastor, I hired a single girl right out of Bible college to work as a secretary and leader over our children's ministry. Her name was Barb. About a year into her employment with us, I noticed her work performance was not what it should be. I noticed she had begun making mistakes that appeared to be from laziness, a lack of skill, or a lack of focus. Several times I called her into my office and tried to talk with her about her life and work. But she seemed aloof, resistant to allowing me to delve too deep, and after each of the meetings her work didn't improve. After about ten meetings like this, I was forced to do something I thought I would never have to do in the ministry. I asked for her resignation.

To my surprise she agreed wholeheartedly and willingly submitted to my request. I told her she was welcome to stay at our church, but she graciously declined, thinking it might be awkward for her to stay. She resigned immediately and left. That is the way she wanted it.

Two months later I received a call from her on a Wednesday night just before our churches' midweek Bible study. She wanted to know if she could come over to my house. She had something to tell me.

I said, "Sure."

She and I sat down in our living room and as she began to cry, this is what she told me.

"Pastor Chris, I am four months pregnant. I couldn't keep going on without telling you. The man is not a Christian, and I don't know if he will marry me or not. But I am so lonely, and I feel so guilty for what I've done. I don't know if God will ever forgive me, and I wouldn't blame you if you didn't. But I couldn't live with myself anymore without telling you the truth."

It was everything I could do to keep from losing all composure. And instantly I understood what had led to her poor performance.

I said, "Barb...oh...Barb, of course I forgive you, and God will forgive you too."

We spent several minutes praying, hugging, crying, and forgiving.

Finally I said, "Barb, will you come back to our church where we can love and support you through this time?"

She asked, "Can I? I didn't think you would let me. I thought you would be so ashamed of me you would never let me come back."

I assured her that wasn't the case. But I told her if she came back, because she had been a staff member when the mistake occurred, she would need to go before the church as it admonishes in 1 Timothy chapter 5.

She agreed.

We were having Sunday night services at the time so we chose the next one for her to stand before the church. I knew no public rebuke needed to take place because she was humble and contrite concerning her sin. But confession on her part was in order.

When she stood up the following Sunday night, I stood beside her supportively. As she began her teary-eyed confession, I could see the awestruck looks on every face in the audience. But as she fumbled through her explanation, I could also see the compassion building in the eyes of her listeners. And when she sobbed out her hope for their forgiveness, I don't think there was a dry eye in the place.

Most of all I sensed God's smile over all that was happening; not for Barb's sin or for the pain she had caused Him or the church. I sensed His smile for the beauty of love His church was displaying as they were poised to forgive and restore this broken life.

When she finished, I asked the people, "Well...what do you think? Do we forgive Barb?"

In one fluid movement, the entire church rose and flocked to the front where Barb and I were standing. I stepped out of the way and watched God's love flow to a broken, hurting, and lonely girl. One by one they hugged her and extended to her, amidst tears of joy, their love, acceptance, and forgiveness.

I wanted to shout so the world could hear, "Do you see the beauty going on here? It's glorious! It's wonderful! And there is no love in the universe that can compare with it. Come on in so you can experience it with us."

Here is why it was so beautiful.

First, the sin she was engaged in was addressed. It wasn't shoved under the carpet, ignored, or denied. It was owned as failure and addressed as transgression before God.

Next, as the scripture in 1 Timothy 5:20 says, the people feared. It wasn't a fear that brought terror. Instead it was the kind that brought a holy awe over the people and reminded them sin lurks in our lives and seeks to destroy. But as we own and confess it, cleansing occurs and God restores.

Finally, a vivid picture was painted for the people that God and His church weren't about judgment, blame, and pointing the finger at wrong doing. It is about forgiving, cleansing, and restoring.

The event actually spoke truth to the church that they could never have heard from a sermon. They could have never captured this message of love from a song sung or a powerful worship time. But they saw firsthand the posture of God concerning our flaws and what the churches' position should be concerning failures in the church, and it was calming, joyous, and uplifting.

The people also saw that when sin is acknowledged and forgiven, it is right, and it is beautiful. We spend our lives trying to hide our sin from God and man—and even ourselves. This creates guilt and a sense of bondage in our minds, characterized by hardness and callousness in our hearts. But when sin is owned, confessed, and humbly laid before God and His people, the environment of forgiveness that is cultivated is delightful to experience. It is delightful as God oversees it, as believers give it, and as the recipient gathers it in.

Last, this kind of pure love, when it happens spontaneously, naturally, and abundantly, is truly beautiful to behold. It fills the air with joy. The atmosphere bubbles with a sense of God's affirming presence and the unity of love all around is absolutely astounding.

Lessons were taught that day and lessons were learned. At the fork in the road, Barb took the correct path. She was tempted to take the wrong one—and for a brief time sauntered in that direction. But she came back to the fork and took the correct path. So did our church.

I think people regularly choose the wrong path at the fork because the correct one looks rocky to start with. As they peer down its expanse, its beginning appears jagged, rough, overgrown, and hard to travel. They sense it is the right path to take, but it looks so laborious and difficult. But it's a faith path. Once one gets by the initial difficulties that go along with confrontation, confession, and humbly placing sin on the table for all to see, there is beauty for the restored and the restorers.

Lisa was afraid to come back to church. She was sure the pastor would hate her. But she and her young daughter were so lonely. And both of them knew deep in their hearts the church they had attended and left several months earlier genuinely loved and cared about them. Lisa especially felt her daughter would flourish at that church because she had made good friends there with children her age who were a part of healthy and godly families. So Lisa decided to risk rejection and shame and take her daughter back there to church.

You see, over a year earlier, Lisa's husband had created an enormous stir in the church. He, Lisa, and their family had come to the area a few years earlier to plant a church. After nearly three years of topsy-turvy results, and being unable to bring together a cohesive group of people, they gave up and came to this church with their shoulders drooping and their heads hanging in defeat.

The church and pastor graciously took them in and quickly found a place for them to serve the body. The pastor even made some adjustments in the church's financial structure to help them as their church-plant experience had left their already struggling financial condition fairly devastated.

Apparently Lisa's husband was hurting more than anyone knew over his inability to make his church-plant work. He dealt with his pain by resorting to some old habits: smoking and drinking. He tried to hide them from everyone, including his wife. But when the elders and church leadership began to smell what they suspected was alcohol on his breath, and did so with increased regularity, they reported it to the pastor. As the reports developed from hearsay into evidence, it became time to approach the couple about the issues that seemed to be reminiscent of a life and family that were hurting and beginning to spin out of control. Also about this time, unknown to Lisa, her husband had approached church leadership with some criticisms he had of the church and the pastor. This escalated the need to confront them as a couple, largely because it seemed her husband was spiraling toward a crash—financially, emotionally, and morally. And it was happening mostly outside of Lisa's awareness.

The pastor and elders approached them gently, lovingly, and supportively offering the church's assistance to help the entire family in whatever way they could—counseling, financially, relationally, etc.

His reaction—he snapped, snarled, and misunderstood. He hauled his family out of church, even though the eight months they had spent there had been incredibly healing for his daughter, his wife, and his two grown children.

Over the next few months, Lisa's husband systematically endeavored to hurt the church as completely as he could by sowing discord among the people in the church through phone calls and sinister visits in anyone's home who would welcome him.

Lisa was caught in the middle because she loved and treasured the church and saw the value it had offered to her family. But her husband was extremely convincing as he described the cruelty of the church's leadership. And she felt obligated to support her husband. So she sat quietly by as he slanderously bashed the church that had been so kind to them.

Until she couldn't take it anymore.

Finally, aware that her husband was indeed on a fast track to a crash and resolved to believe what her gut was telling her rather than what her husband was telling her, she separated from her husband and took her daughter with her. They secured an apartment together, and with Lisa's steady job determined to make a life on their own.

One day, after they had tried several churches following the separation, Lisa and her little girl drove by the old church.

Her daughter said, "Mommy, I want to go back to our old church. That's where I had the most fun and the most friends. I don't like any of these other churches. Why can't we just go there?"

Lisa knew in her heart that she too had loved her time there. And she knew it would be a healthy place for her daughter. Yet, she was sure the pastor and leadership would hate her and reject her.

Finally, on a Sunday morning a few weeks after her daughter's request, she was late getting her tiny fragmented family ready in time to visit a church she had picked out on the other side of town.

Her daughter began to pester her, "Mommy, can we go to our old church? Please? I don't want to go to any other churches. I don't like any of them. And our old church is really close. We can get there on time easy."

Lisa took a deep breath and said, "OK."

However, when they pulled into the parking lot and walked into the front entrance, Lisa froze. The service was about to begin, and the foyer was empty. She stood there next to her daughter all alone, unable to move.

"Mommy, what's the matter?"

But Lisa felt she had no right to be in this church—the one that had loved them toward wholeness—and the one her and her husband had returned the favor to by trying to destroy it.

As she stood there about ready to do an about-face and run out the door, a member of the leadership team walked by and recognized her. He went right over to her and welcomed her and her little girl with an exuberant embrace.

"Lisa...how good to see you. How are you?" He said.

Lisa received the welcome appreciatively but still felt she was unworthy to penetrate the church facility any further.

Lisa asked, "Would you go and ask pastor if it is all right for my daughter and I to come to church this morning?"

"Well sure it's OK." He said.

"Would you please go and ask him?" Lisa insisted.

So the elder went into the sanctuary, tapped the pastor on the shoulder, and said, "There is someone in the foyer who wants to ask you something."

The pastor looked a bit puzzled.

"Come and see." The elder prodded.

When the pastor came around the corner and saw Lisa and her daughter, a big smile formed on his face, tears flooded his eyes, and he walked straight toward the two ladies with his arms wide open.

He wrapped his arms around both of them as he said, "I am so glad to see you. I have been worried about you."

Lisa was glad for the welcome. She sensed her sins being washed and forgiven even as his arms were being gathered around her and her daughter.

But she still couldn't move.

She straightened her posture, wiped her teary eyes and asked, "Pastor, I wonder if you would let me and my daughter come to your church this morning? I would understand completely if you said no."

"How silly, Lisa," the pastor said. "Of course you can come. In fact, I want you to sit right next to me during the worship time."

The next week Lisa stood before the church, at her request, and confessed the sin of divisiveness and asked for forgiveness. When she finished her humble and tear-filled confession, the entire church rose to embrace her and confirm their and God's love for her.

My read on this kind of moment is that there is nothing more beautiful in all of Christendom. All the traits of spiritual beauty are there. I have never seen a majestic stallion, a strikingly attractive woman, a stunning sunset, or a captivating mountain landscape that could ever come close in beauty to a scene such as this in a healthy and loving church.

We've all fantasized about being an eagle and soaring above a breathtaking mountain view and basking in the freedom such an experience would give. But if you want to soar spiritually, be the type of person or church that is ready to restore.

To put it another way, if you want to see real beauty, don't be rigid or judgmental or postured to make people tow the line—or pay a price for their failures. Instead, position your heart to reflect God's heart and be poised to restore.

THE LOVE KILLERS

There is not one church in the world that is exempt from violations against the law of love. I am talking about violations like gossip, criticism, unforgiveness, dissention, insubordination, jealousy between members, discord sowing, and so forth. Any church is susceptible to any of these blights on the law of love. I call them the love killers.

Some people actually feel it is normal for churches to have these kinds of skirmishes going on because they make church life interesting. *Interesting* is an interesting choice of words because they don't make life interesting. They make it grievous. They cripple the life flow of God's love in a fellowship, making the church a place where battles are fought, rather than a place where love is wrought and sinners are caught. They kill love—dead.

I know of two pastors who are simply resolved in their hearts that the environment of church must be skirmish-free—no love killers allowed. One of these churches has an attendance of eleven hundred and the other one hundred and fifty. One is on the west coast and the other in the east. One is casual, the other more traditional. So they are very different.

Yet, whenever these pastors catch wind of a gossipy rumor, a criticism of any kind, unforgiveness between members, dissention in the ranks, or any other potential love-killing behavior in their churches, in like manner they promptly call the person or persons responsible into their offices. And they calmly go through a loving, but firm and simple confrontation routine. Their reason for doing this isn't paranoia. It isn't fear or a weak self-concept. They don't feel threatened or that their church won't survive a little tension. Their reasons stem solely from Scripture. They use these scriptures as their authority. "Endeavoring to keep the Spirit of unity in the bond of peace" (Eph. 4:3). "Reprove, rebuke, exhort with all long suffering" (2 Tim. 4:2, KJV). "Cast out the scoffer, and contention will leave; Yes, strife and reproach will cease" (Prov. 22:10). "Reject a divisive man after the first and second admonition" (Titus 3:10). "Those who are sinning rebuke...that the rest also may fear." (1 Tim. 4:20). "Warn those who are unruly" (1 Thess. 5:14).

The routine goes something like this. After a few preliminary conversation starters about how they are doing or how the kids are getting along, they begin. "Hey, thanks for coming, Sam. Listen, I just wanted to check something out with you. A couple of days ago I caught wind of a rumor that you said this and that about so and so. I just wanted to find out from you if that was true. I figured the best way to do that was to talk to you directly."

- Sometimes the person refuses to own up to the rumor and denies the whole thing.

- Sometimes the person owns up to it, but clarifies what he or she actually said.

- Sometimes the person admits the whole thing, and they have a discussion about the content of the rumor and the right or wrongness of talking amongst the sheep.

- Sometimes, but seldom, the person stomps out of the office and the church.

- Sometimes the person apologizes and asks for forgiveness.

But here is what always happens. The person goes away from the meeting knowing that leadership feels it is not acceptable to talk freely about these kinds of things. It stamps a clear imprint on the person's heart that this church does not condone any kind of love-killing communication going on in and among its members. When people know a law of love violation will generate a visit to a pastor's or elder's office, they are less likely to talk about these kinds of things. If the Scripture is correct (and it is), they will possess a godly fear that will cause them to think twice about engaging in the dissenting transgression again.

Throughout the Bible, God never granted permission for His people to engage in the love killers. In fact, whenever they did, they received His fiercest wrath. (See Numbers 12:1, 9–10; 14:29; 16:41–46; 21:5–6.)

Always, an attitude that kills love needs to leave the church, no exceptions. Sometimes the attitude in the person leaves, which is the objective of this kind of confrontation. But if the person refuses to allow the attitude to leave his or her heart, it is the difficult task of leadership to ask the person with the love-killing attitude to leave the church. It is unfortunate, but the Scripture and the law of love demand it. Just a side note, this doesn't need to be the task of the pastor. Elders or a Senior Staff Pastor can perform this function. However, it should proceed from the heart of the point leader of the church.

Both of the churches these two pastors lead enjoy and maintain a sweet spirit of unity in their fellowships. Do the love killers stay away completely? No, they surface from time to time. But they are dealt with immediately. Do these leaders enjoy confronting? Absolutely not! It's just something they know they need to do if they are to maintain the kind of unity the Bible says we are supposed to have in our churches.

The pastor's role in any church includes the title, Care-taker of Community. And it's not just for unity in the church. Jesus said (my paraphrase), "Love one another that all men might know that you are my disciples" (John 13:35). That tells us the task of loving one another has evangelistic implications. So that if a pastor endeavors "to keep the spirit of unity in the bond of peace" (Eph. 4:3), he is also, at least in part, being obedient to Jesus' instruction about evangelism. Furthermore, indirectly, he is obeying Paul's admonition to Pastor Timothy to "do the work of an evangelist" (2 Tim. 4:5). I am sure doing the work of an evangelist includes more. But I don't think it is a stretch to say that the pastor who strives to maintain an atmosphere of love in his church is also maintaining an environment where evangelism can occur. He is engaging in evangelism-friendly work.

Since so many pastors struggle to keep the fires of evangelism alive in their churches and people, confronting the love killers is a practical way to keep those fires burning.

There are so many huge mountainous types of difficulties that can emerge in churches where the love killers have begun to take hold. And those mountains will become more rugged and more problematic to scale if they are left unaddressed. They grow like volcanoes and have the potential to explode with destructive and disastrous results.

Do you remember the eagle I talked about a few minutes ago?

A few years back I was with a buddy of mine on a camping trip in the mountains of Colorado. As you may know, the view is breathtaking. We were camping at an elevation of about eighty-five hundred feet and all around us were peaks along the tops of ridges that rose to eleven and twelve thousand feet.

At one point my friend pointed above us and said, "Do you see that bird flying up there? That is a golden eagle."

I leaned my head back, placed my binoculars on my face between my eyes and the bird and asked, "How do you know it is a golden eagle and not just a hawk?"

As I continued to spy the majestic creature soar above us he said, "One thing is its size. But you can also tell by the shape of the markings on the underside of its wings. And you know it isn't a bald eagle because its head and tail aren't white."

I looked closer and, sure enough, the bird was deep brown in color; but there were some distinct lighter colored markings under its wings that were different from any other bird I had ever seen.

Then, no sooner had I spotted the markings, but the giant bird swirled around a few times in the updrafts, rose quickly in elevation, and disappeared over one of the twelve-thousand-foot-high peaks above us. It was beautiful and awe-inspiring to behold.

The church with the courage to address it, and which is obedient to God's admonition to "keep the spirit of unity in the bond of peace" will take its people above the seemingly impossible to scale rugged and dangerous mountains created by the love killers. They will seem as mountains do to the eagle—no problem to get over at all. They may lurk as potential peaks of concern, but will not have a place in your fellowship because they are being lovingly and responsibly addressed. As this happens, you and your church will simply soar above the problems.

It will be a thing of majestic beauty. And morally, your church and your people will begin to foster an environment that will feel like the crisp cleanness of high mountain air and the beauty of an eagle soaring peacefully and effortlessly above the rugged kinds of difficulties that other people and churches don't know how to get over.

Chapter 10

~

Constrained to Love

THERE REALLY IS no subject that Jesus addressed more than love. He attacked people's inabilities to love or compulsions to do its opposite from every angle.

- He challenged anger (Matt. 5:22).

- He addressed hatred (Luke 6:27).

- He implored people to forgive (Matt. 18:21–22).

- He challenged judgementalism (Matt. 7:1–5).

- He prohibited revenge (Matt. 5:38–42).

- He encouraged reconciliation (Matt. 5:23–26).

- He discouraged racial prejudice (Luke 9: 52–56).

- He instructed his followers to go as far as to love their enemies (Matt. 5:44).

- He made it the only command we are required
  to keep, save loving God (Matt. 22:37–40).

And I could go on. It is clear Jesus placed paramount
importance on the need for people to love.

But more important than His admonitions to love, was
that He Himself was love in human form. He came to earth
as a bundle of love on the first Christmas. He loved purely
and completely everyone He came in contact with on earth
for His entire life. Then He put on the greatest display of love
the world has ever seen—or will ever see—when He went to
the cross. Jesus didn't talk love; He was love.

In 2 Corinthians 5:14 (KJV) it tells us that "the love of Christ
constraineth us." That means it controls us. It restrains us. It
holds us back from expressing hatred, anger, judgment, and
criticism. And it compels us to give more, serve more, assist
more, and love more than our flesh may want to. In a person
or a church, an abundance of this kind of love is invaluable
and beautiful.

One day when I was a pastor of a church in Boulder, Colorado, I came home from a day at work and learned that the
neighbor across the street from our house had come to my
door about an hour before I arrived home and berated my
wife because our dog had been barking too much.

For a few years when our youngest son was growing
up, at his pleading, we acquired a dog for him. As our son
grew older, he became less interested in the dog and the pet
became ours. But we only had the one, and because both my
wife and I were gone all days most days, our canine became
lonely and started barking at everyone and everything that
went by. We didn't know about his barking until this man
dumped his truckload of resentment on my wife.

Shirley had been gone part of the day as well. Apparently the neighbor was waiting and watching, because she had no more entered the house and placed her purse on the table, but there was a knock on the door. When she answered it, our neighbor began to scream at her for our insensitivity to allow our dog to disturb our whole neighborhood.

He shouted. He screamed. He swore. He belittled her and shamed her. He was outright cruel and frightening to her. When he left and she turned from the door, so emotionally aroused was she over the man's fury, she was shaking in fright, and she began to cry.

When I arrived home and she informed me of the incident, I was livid. I was so angry, I began to shake. I thought, "What nerve he had treating my wife in that way. At least have the backbone to wait until the man arrives home. Don't go and pick on the lady of the house to the point of cursing at her and frightening her to tears."

Honestly, I wanted to ravage the man's face.

I paced in our living room for about fifteen minutes firing myself up and rehearsing what I was going to say to him. Then I burst through our front door and headed straight across the street for our neighbor's house.

But in the short walk from our front door to his, God spoke to me. He planted five thoughts in my head.

- First, "You are a pastor over my sheep and a Christian. You don't have the Holy Spirit's permission to do what you are about to do."

- Second, "The man you are about to attack is not a Christian. He doesn't have access to the Spirit to lead him to be kind as you do."

- Third, "He is compelled by his nature to berate, while you are constrained to love."

- Fourth, "Cast coals of fire on him by loving him." (See Romans 12:20.)

- Fifth, "A soft answer turns away wrath" (Prov. 15:1).

Don't ask me how this much analysis and dialogue between God and I went through my head in such a short amount of time. But it did.

When he opened the door, I could see the fight in his face as well. He was seething, breathing hard, and armed for bear.

I said, "I am so sorry our dog has been disturbing you. We didn't realize he was doing that much barking. Please forgive us. We will try to resolve the situation."

I remember feeling as though I was outside of myself listening to my words as I spoke. "Is that me talking?" I seemed to ask myself. "That's not what I want to say. You're blowing it—blowing it! Say what you were going to say. Let this guy have it. He deserves it."

But God wouldn't let me.

In four short sentences, I watched the glare in his eyes, the snarl in his lips, and the fight in his countenance soften to apologetic gentleness.

He responded, "I guess it's not that bad. I probably came down too hard on your wife. I'm sorry for coming on so strong."

And that was it.

I agreed to work on our dog. He agreed to work on his tolerance. We shook hands and it was over. It was an incredible result, and it speaks of the power and effectiveness of living God's word. But it wasn't over for me. I was still angry, but not at my neighbor. I was angry at God.

For several days I pouted. I did so because in Christ I don't have the freedom to let people like my neighbor have it, as he let my wife have it.

I was mad. I told God, "My neighbor can say anything he wants. If he is angry he can cuss, rant, rave, shout, scream, and be just as obnoxious as he wants because he doesn't answer to a constraining Holy Spirit. But I don't have that freedom. It's not fair, and I don't like it.

"Furthermore," I told the Lord, "why do I have these kinds of emotions in the first place if I can't express them? And why in Your word do You want me as a husband to nourish, cherish, and protect my wife; but when I am ready to be obedient to those directives that You have given, You say no?"

I really did have it out with God.

I resolved my issues with Him rather quickly. No doubt, the great results that day helped. But the whole incident alerted me to a reality in Christian loving. It is this. God wants us to live out and demonstrate His love to others. He wants us to do it victoriously and completely, and He makes no apologies for it. And to insure we do it, He has commissioned His Holy Spirit to pull back the reigns—to restrain us—to constrain and control our out of control emotions.

There are many areas where God's constraining love is at work in our lives. I would like to talk about a few.

LOVING ENEMIES

One Sunday at the end of the service, a pastor of a church asked his congregation, "How many of you have forgiven your enemies?"

Only about half raised their hands.

He asked the question a second time.

In response, this time about 75 percent of the people held up their hands.

So he asked the question a third time, and this time the whole church raised their hands except one tiny elderly lady.

The minister asked, "Mrs. Jenkins, aren't you willing to forgive your enemies?"

"I don't have any enemies," the lady responded sweetly.

"Mrs. Jenkins, that is very unusual. How old are you?" he asked.

"Ninety-four," she replied.

"I'm so impressed, Mrs. Jenkins," the preacher said. "What a great example you are to us. Would you be so kind as to come here to the front of our church this morning and share with us how you have been able to live ninety-four years and not have even one enemy in the whole world?"

The sweet lady carefully hobbled down the isle, turned to face the church and said, "I outlived the witches."

The idea of this story, as well as the way Jesus addressed the issue, reminds us we all have enemies. Some we have earned. Some we haven't. Some we know about. Some we don't. But most likely each of us has an enemy of some kind somewhere.

One of mine was convinced I told his wife to leave him. I didn't, mind you. He was abusive to her verbally, emotionally, and physically. I might have advised it, at least temporarily, for her safety, but I never got that far with her. Yet when she left him, he was convinced I had told her to do so. I tried to assure him I hadn't, but no amount of convincing would change his mind. And so I have an enemy.

As a result, he spread some awful lies about me to others in an attempt to hurt me in the same way he surmised I had hurt him. He even threatened to me and others to take my life. And over the years, I have desired to hate him in return for all of the false rumors he spread and the grief he caused me personally. But God won't let me.

Here is what happens in my life when I am tempted to hate someone for an offence someone did to me. When I go to prayer about the incident, I will tell God why I need to hang onto my feelings about this person. When I do, the Holy Spirit pricks my heart and says something like, "You can't hate this man. That would not please me." Then the Lord will remind me, "Besides, you know about the anger issues and blame issues in his life that would cause him to point his finger at you. You have to be compassionate and merciful."

Then when I read the Bible, it seems as if every passage about loving my enemies stands out like a flashing neon light—love your enemies, love this person, let it go, and thus fulfill the law of Christ. (See Matthew 5:44; Romans 13:8–10; Galatians 6:2.)

In short, the Holy Spirit constrains us to love. There may be a hundred other chains and bonds we must shed at all costs. But the Holy Spirit's constraint on us to love must not be resisted. It is what God has placed upon us to keep His beauty on display and to help make us truly free.

ANGER

Another example of God's love constraining us is in an area of universal difficulty—anger. I have found that God's love is constantly constraining me concerning the anger issues that would like to surface in my life. Sometimes I can almost feel Him holding me back, saying to me, "Slow down, Chris. Take it easy. Take a deep breath."

My whole life I have played basketball. I played in junior high, high school, college, city leagues, and pick-up games. While I was pastor of a church in Southern California, a couple of mornings a week before work I played with a group of Christians in the gym of a small Christian college in the area.

There was a man in the group of guys I played with whose name was Jeff. After a month or so, he started getting a little rough with me—throwing elbows, extra pushing, a little tripping, and a lot of attitude. I started to wonder, "What's with this guy? Does he have a problem with me or something? I mean after all, what's not to like?" After a few more weeks of the same abuse, that seemed to be aimed only at me, I started to feel really angry and that I didn't like him very much either. It was probably a testosterone thing, but it was real nonetheless.

The next week, working up to the day when I would go back and play again, I thought, "Forget it, I just won't go back." Or the next day I'd think, "I haven't done anything to this guy, I'll just ignore him." Or at the office, I would become upset and think, "If he causes me grief, I'll just get right back in his face." I was really tormented by the whole thing.

But all of that self-talk was simply God's love constraining me.

The night before I was to go back to play, God tightened his grip on my spirit and impressed upon me, "You need to go to him tomorrow and get it right. You need to let go of the anger you feel and love this guy. You're a big boy. You can do this."

So I determined to do it. But, you guessed it, I didn't like it. In the back of my mind, I was telling myself, "You didn't do anything to start this thing. It wasn't your issue. He's the one with the problem. He should come to you." Everything in me wanted to give my anger its way.

But God won.

The next day I arrived early and waited outside the front entrance for Jeff to come. When he did I pulled him aside.

I said, "Jeff, listen. It's obvious something has gotten between us. I don't know where it came from, but I know it's there. And my attitude has been rotten. I'm sorry for whatever I did to perpetuate this thing. I don't want anything to be between us. Will you forgive me?"

The whole time I was talking with him, he looked at me with suspicion. But as he saw I was sincere, he softened his hard exterior and responded, "Well, my attitude hasn't been very good either, I guess. I'm sorry for being a jerk. Let's put it behind us."

And just like that it was gone.

It is because the Holy Spirit constrains us to love and restrains us in the expression of our anger.

All of us who know Christ have a fleshly (or carnal) and a spiritual side. If left uninfluenced by God's Spirit, our fleshly side will always try to pull us "south" toward hatred, angry feelings, and outbursts. Our flesh will tug and prod us to have "ought" with our brothers, sisters, fellow church members, family members, fellow employees, boss, or whoever. (See Matthew 5:23.) And it will do so, convincing us of a thousand good reasons for why we should never love the person and resolve the angry feelings between us.

There is something I have noticed in movies and television dramas. When an anger issue arises in a story and the actors become angry or heated, often they say the exact thing our flesh would want us to say. But these actors don't say it awkwardly or in a fumbling manner as we would if we said it in a real life situation. No. The theme of the story and the directors have the actors poised to deliver their angry monologues in perfect fashion. They play up the moment with precise timing. The music builds. There is a drum roll. The hated person in the story is the recipient and the star is the deliverer of the angry words—and speaks them in just the right manner to humiliate the despised character. Then the star will walk out, slam the door behind him, having put the other person in his place—leaving the audience with the impression that anger is the right thing to express and the correct thing to feel. We just need to be in control enough to say it the right way.

It all just glamorizes anger. We are impressed with the way anger is expressed on the television screen, and we go away thinking angry and heated confrontations are good things.

We do the same thing in our self-talk scenarios. We will drive down the freeway, and when someone cuts us off, we will start to rehearse scenarios where we find ourselves in angry conversations with the person that just committed the vehicular assault on us. And in the rehearsal, we are articulate. We are in control. We are right, the wording is perfect, and the errant driver is adequately humiliated. But it is just make believe.

We will go away from those unreal dramatizations, whether on television or in our minds, thinking our destructive anger is right and good. Furthermore, it fires up our flesh so that it is harder to hear God when He attempts to constrain us with His love.

The reality is that if we find ourselves in a potentially volatile conversation, seldom do we say things correctly. We

150

usually stumble over our words. Or we alienate the people we talk to with clumsy and hateful remarks. Or we misconstrue the situation so that our verbal jabs aren't even accurate. And all the while—for Christians anyway—God is speaking to us and trying to pull back the reigns on our angry passions. He is trying to restrain our tongues and our attitudes. He is constraining us to love instead of hate—to let Him reign in our spirits instead of allowing them to be out of control. He will try to get us to let it go, reconcile, or win our brother or sister. It is one of the busiest, most widespread functions of the Holy Spirit. He constrains us to love and to do so with His love radiating through us.

There are several reasons Jesus implores us to love each other, just as there are several reasons for why the Holy Spirit is constantly trying to impress upon our hearts to love. And there are many reasons for why the love of Christ is forever about the task of constraining us. But here is one reason that is obvious—so obvious none of us needs to be a brain surgeon to figure it out.

God's plan is that we would become like Christ. (See Romans 8:29.)

God wants the hearts of each of His followers, and I believe the environments of each gathering of His church, to be saturated with the love of God—His pure love, His genuine love, His divine love, His healing, encouraging, uplifting, life transforming, and life-infusing love; so that we would be like Him.

Have you ever been in the presence of a child of God who is truly compelled to love? There are plenty of them around. You just have to look for them. Every collection of His church has several, some more than others. These people are loving, joyful, peaceful, patient, kind, faithful, and filled with meekness and self-control. (See Galatians 5:22.) They are accepting and nonjudgmental. They are gracious and humble, wise, and filled with the mercy of God. And all manner of people—sinners and saints, children and adults alike—can feel God's love in their hearts. They aren't perfect, but they have a special bond with the One who is.

My advice is, find out who they are and be like them. Follow them as they follow Christ. (See 1 Corinthians 11:1.) Upgrade the model you choose to pattern yourself after in your Christian walk. If you have been following the example of a Christian who is less loving and less of an example than the persons I described in the previous paragraph, keep that one as a friend but lose the person as a model.

The Christian who is constrained to love—and the church that has ever increasing numbers who are constrained to love—is on a course to bring the beauty of heaven right into their presence.

Chapter 11

❧

Indigenous Love

RECENTLY, AFTER NEARLY forty years of ministry, my wife and I moved back to our hometown in Western New York. Shirley's family had some land available, and out of generosity and respect for the ministry, they gave us two acres of land in the country on which we could build a home.

As we watched our house come together, Shirley decided she wanted to decorate the planters around our new home with rocks that were indigenous to the area. So we began to scour the countryside for natural rocks. But as we searched, we found we didn't like the looks of the natural rocks around our house. They were flat and smooth and gray and dull in appearance and really quite unimpressive. We had just moved from the Colorado area where it seemed that every rock we came across was large, round, colorful, and prime for landscaping. The bad news was that it seemed every rock you could find in Colorado was protected in some way by law. Either they were labeled as city or county property, or they were a part of a park or national forest and taking them would deface the land. In New York, however, the country-side was littered with these ugly rocks, and no one cared how many you took.

In the end, we concluded we didn't like the indigenous rocks at all. We decided to go with an entirely different land-scaping idea all together.

We did not have indigenous love.

If that doesn't confuse you concerning the title of this chapter, let me see if I can confound you further on the subject.

I attended a conference once where an instructor talked about studies that had been done when the church growth movement was strong in America and around the world concerning the effect like-people groups had on church growth. He reported to us that it was discovered that churches in certain ethnic areas of cities, regions, or states that were primarily filled with people of like ethnic origin—as long as they adhered to other church growth principles—were more likely to see their fellowships grow.

In short the studies were saying that if a church in a certain ethnic area was made up largely of people also in the same area and ethnicity, it created a comfortable environment for the people of that church. If that happened, that church would be more likely to experience growth.

He made apologies for this, citing that it sounded a lot like willing segregation for the sake of church growth, but that studies don't lie. It softened the results, however, when they gave examples of churches that seemed to be excep-tions to the rule. They told of churches that had mixed racial constituents, but had other unifying factors that made them indigenous.

I recall the instructor saying that a church in one of the studies had a mixed racial constituency, but the church's financial or class status seemed to suggest another unifying denominator. The church was filled with doctors, lawyers, and executives who all seemed to possess an indigenous kind of relationship. The people were all middle- to upper-class and above. And this church grew, the study said, because the thread of commonality was money.

Another church was given as an example by this same instructor; it was also filled with a mixture of races, but the indigenous factor was a blue collar class system. The people of different races seemed to work for the same types of manufacturing companies. They were united by their relationship with each other at their respective places of employment and their oneness of understanding concerning their middle-class job status and monetary culture. This church was growing, they said, because the indigenous factor uniting them was their blue collar culture, not their ethnic sameness.

Again, the growth people apologized because it looked a lot like segregation, but said if you want your church to grow, you need to have some kind of a cultural indigenous flavor that would seep through the ethnic cracks in the fellowship.

These churches didn't have indigenous love either.

By now you must be thoroughly baffled. So let me confuse you at one more additional level before I bring this all together.

Another discovery was made along these lines about missions work.

It was always the strategy of missions in years, decades, and even centuries gone by that missionaries sent to foreign countries and people groups should be the primary presenters and modelers of the gospel message. If a work grew and more workers were needed, as long as there was money to fund their ministry, additional missionaries should be raised up and sent from the country that sent the first missionaries. This was assumed because, in their thinking, only truly redeemed and culturally transformed people could set an example proper enough to influence the kind of transformation desired for the evangelized people groups. This was the feeling, and for decades—even centuries—missionary endeavors from developed countries like England and the United States were structured this way.

There were a few smaller denominations, however, which were poorly funded and meagerly staffed that could not afford to send missionaries when a work grew. So they resorted to a taboo practice. They decided to raise up leadership from the people they evangelized to lead their growing missionary endeavors. This was done for many years, and the works continued to grow and abound. They were called indigenous missionary works.

It was only a few decades ago that it dawned on someone that the indigenous missionary works were growing larger and faster than any of the other conventional outreaches. And they were doing so in spite of the fact that funding was still poor and quantities of workers from the mother countries remained minimal.

It was discovered that the small, poorly funded and staffed denominations had stumbled onto the mission's discovery of the millennium. Indigenous missionary endeavors are the most effective and are part of God's plan for the growth of His church.

What does this have to do with indigenous love? Let me explain.

God's Word makes an incredible claim about Christian love, one that no other religious persuasion can fully embrace, reproduce, or understand.

Galatians 3:28 says, "There is neither Jew nor Greek, there is neither slave nor free, there is neither male nor female; for you are all one in Christ."

This scripture absolutely amazes me!

The verse encompasses every ethnic difference, every class difference, and every gender difference. It is not saying Jews should love Greeks or whites should love blacks. It is not saying Christians should have more tolerance for women, Asians, and poor people.

The verse is saying, "In Christ the differences don't exist."

God sees no difference. So if we are in Christ, we should see no difference. God looks not upon the outward appearance, but upon the heart; we should do the same. (See 1 Samuel 16:7.) God loves all the same—we should love all the same.

Indigenous love (at least according to my definition) is love that flows naturally out of a believer who has been transformed by the pure love of God for every class, religious, ethnic, and gender difference, accepting each as completely as one would another of his or her own group. It is indigenous because it grows out of God's heart that is naturally attached to and deeply in love with every person of every culture. Then it flows out of newly rejuvenated hearts that have been transformed by His Holy Spirit.

At a minister's meeting in a multicultural west coast city, a young pastor of one ethnicity sat at a table of pastors of the same ethnicity, except for one who was of another race. I was at the table as well. The pastor of the other race was older and led a church almost completely made up of people from his own race. The young pastor led a church made up of all different races.

The young pastor was a little unpolished and inexperienced in matters of the world. Though he was pastor of a church in a multicultural city, he was born and had lived his entire adolescent years in a small town that had no ethnic diversity whatsoever. It seemed this fact, rather than causing him to be bigoted as a result of his ignorance, made him accepting of all races because he was untainted by worldly influences. This seems the case, because he found himself leading and loving people from five or six different ethnic representations in a church that found his own race in the strong minority.

The older pastor of a different race had a vast array of knowledge and experiences, which in the real world was endless. He was a self-appointed spokesman in the Christian community in his area for racial equality and unity.

The week before it just so happened that the churches of these two pastors had played a softball game against each other. The older pastor wasn't at the ballgame but the younger pastor was. At the table that day, at a certain point, the younger got the attention of the older and began to lavish praise on the people from the older pastor's church.

The younger pastor said something like, "What a great time we had. The people from your church were some of the nicest people I have ever met. It was obvious they really loved the Lord. It was the first time I have ever done anything like that with anyone from a church from one ethnic persuasion. What a joy it was to fellowship with them. It was a new and delightful experience for me."

The older pastor became very quiet. Anyone watching him could see he was brewing, thinking, analyzing, examining the young pastor's words.

Finally after about five minutes, the older, experienced, seasoned pastor quieted the table, looked at the young pastor, and said, "I thought I heard you just say, 'You didn't know that people of my race could love the Lord like they did.'"

You could see the young pastor was taken aback. It was apparent he wasn't sure where the seasoned pastor was coming from, unsure whether the older man was making a joke, on the verge of returning the compliment, or seriously confronting him because he stammered and wound up saying, "I'm not sure…I guess…is that what I said?"

I knew it wasn't what he had said. But it was the way the older pastor had interpreted it.

The older pastor said with anger and clarity in front of the seven other pastors at the table, "That was the stupidest, most inconsiderate remark I have ever heard."

With that the older pastor pushed his chair back, rose to his feet, and stomped out of the room.

The younger pastor sat there shaking, embarrassed, devastated.

The other pastors at the table who knew the older pastor better than the younger one, tried to comfort the younger fledgling church leader.

"He's like that sometimes. He thinks he is the protector of his race from all attacks. What you said was wonderful. You have no reason to feel bad about what you said. He always misinterprets things."

However, I could see their words of comfort were not making a difference. This young pastor was shaken.

As soon as the dinner meeting was over, the young man said his goodbyes and made a beeline for his car. He told me later, as soon as he got into his vehicle and closed the door he burst into tears. When his tears subsided he drove off, but his cries continued to resurface all the way home.

Later, the younger man made all the phone calls and scheduled the get-together with the older pastor to seek reconciliation. He was the one who apologized. He was the one who asked forgiveness. He was the one who learned a lesson and changed from the incident.

It was my observation that the older pastor, who had made it his life-long task to improve race relations, was the more racially charged and disobedient to God of the two men. He not only saw differences in the two of them, he invented racial issues that weren't there. It made me feel that all he had done over the years to assist our society in bringing about racial equality was tainted by a heart that didn't really understand the heart of God in the matter.

Yet, the younger pastor was the closest to the indigenous love of God I had ever seen. Yes, perhaps he was a bit free with what he had said. But all of us at the table could see he had a sincere, almost colorblind, loving heart for the people of the other pastor's church. Furthermore, he had a church that reflected his heart. He was a man filled with indigenous love.

When Christians (especially a church full of them) have the love of God so living through their hearts that they don't even consider differences as they offer their love—that is indigenous love. When it flows so fluidly that love and acceptance for people of any culture, class, position in society or ethnicity is not even noticed—that is indigenous love. When church growth factors, the opinions of others, or the cultural and racial structures of our society are shunned in favor of pleasing the heart of God—that is indigenous love. When we don't have to stand up and tell people to love their red, yellow, black, brown, and white brothers and sisters—that is indigenous love.

And need I say it is one of the most beautiful sights in His church.

I am proud to say my wife's and my own dearest friends are from five racial origins, including my own Caucasian background. I didn't set out to make friends from these ethnic groups. I didn't target them because I wanted to be able to say I had friends from these diverse races. It just happened. It happened as naturally as ducks adapt to water and eagles to flight. They aren't our token friends. They are our dearest and most trusted friends. I trust their intelligence. I trust their wisdom. I trust their spirituality, their maturity, their advice, and their love for us.

It is one of the beautiful blessings of my life.

If someone tried to say to me, "If you have a mixture of people like that in your church, you can expect to see minimal church growth;" if someone said, "With diversity such as this in your ministry you may not receive favor from certain organizations, groups, or lending agencies;" if someone said, "Your effectiveness in our culture may suffer because of the assorted groups you have in your ministry," I would stand and shout from the housetops, "Bring on the suffering, the lack of growth and the persecution!" Because deep in my heart I know God's smile is over me for the indigenous love stand I have made.

It is beautiful to know the bright and affirming laughter of God shines upon you because His indigenous love is living through you.

Chapter 12

✦

The "One Anothers"

IT IS NO small doctrine in the Bible. Loving one another is an admonition that was introduced in the book of Genesis and was repeated with direct or indirect mention in almost every book in the Bible, straight through the book of Revelation.

It is also a primary theme in the ministry of Jesus. He said, "This is my commandment, that you love one another as I have loved you" (John 15:12). "By this all will know that you are My disciples, if you have love for one another" (John 13:35). "On these two commandments [loving God and neighbor] hang all the Law and the Prophets" (Matt. 22:40). "These things I command you, that you love one another" (John 15:17).

By the time the concept had gotten into Paul's heart, it had become a major component to the continued cohesiveness of the churches he launched and eventually established in the faith with his writings. When Jesus' and Paul's references to the "one anothers" are dissected and fully applied, a remarkable sense of loving beauty is unleashed in the church of Jesus Christ.

All of the "one anothers" deal at the root level with a different aspect of love. Each touches on a subject that, if they could be woven together into a single proverbial cloth, would form the most beautiful, the most pure, and the most complete tapestry of love that exists in the entire universe. In this chapter I want to show you a few components of this tapestry and how they come together to reveal the beauty of God's love in His church.

Unfortunately, every aspect of our society—especially in our American culture—resists, from both an environmental and a temporal level, the components of this beauty. We are too busy to love one another. What with our kids entering into every sports and extracurricular activity in town; and both mom and dad having to work to make ends meet; and with the demands companies place on their employees in order for them to keep their jobs; and with the requirements, or at least requests, the church places on its members to "work for Jesus"; who has time to love each other anymore? It is an ever-increasing struggle fighting against the norms our society has come to follow.

Just ten years ago when my youngest son was in his mid-teens, our family strained to keep a semblance of functional and biblical structure. Many of his friends were a part of single-parent or blended families whose parents all worked, and in some cases, worked different shifts. Just getting our son home at a regular time for supper on a daily basis was a challenge, because few of his friends had a similar structure to adhere to. And that was ten years ago. It is worse today.

Every Christian value, such as family gatherings, family devotions, church involvement, traditional family structures, time to reflect, instruct, model, and just hang out, is becoming more and more difficult to accomplish.

It doesn't mean we should cave into the pressure and go with the flow of the secular retreat away from Christian norms and values. On the contrary, we should fight against the current and prevail. But the reality is that more and more families are caving. This makes it even more difficult, value-wise, to love one another as the Scripture encourages. People protect their privacy with greater vigor. They don't understand the value of speaking truth to one another. It is becoming a greater emotional and functional leap for people to love one another, forgive one another, confess faults to one another, and fellowship with one another than it ever was before. If we thought it was a struggle to do these things twenty-five years ago, it is even more that way today.

But when Christians and churches are able to navigate through the cultural and societal evolutionary digressions of our age and accomplish the "one anothers," people are still amazed by God's love in the hearts of His people and are attracted to its beauty.

ADMONITION

In Romans 15:14 and Colossians 3:16, Paul exhorts his Christ-followers to admonish one another. Admonish means "warn, exhort, urge, caution, and reprove." Related scriptures are, "Speaking the truth in love" (Eph. 4:15), and "Exhort one another" (Heb. 3:13).

This may be the most difficult of all the "one anothers" to practice because trust, as well as time to build trust, are so elusive today. Even in our most functional homes, the pressures from our society to protect our home turf, hide the truth, project false fronts, and guard our fragile self-esteems from attack seem to get filtered into the mindsets of most individuals. So that it is a bigger leap for people to be transparent, bear their hearts, and be honest about faults than ever before. Even people called into the ministry are coming into Christ's service with greater and more complicated assortments of emotional baggage. But when some of these separating walls are torn down, and people can begin to trust enough to give and receive challenge, exhortation, and admonition—in an environment of Christian love—it is a beautiful thing.

Robert M., Wes S., and I had such a group. There were just three of us and we were all pastors, so we were also peers. We were also close to each other in age, so our life's experiences were similar. Culturally, two of us were Anglo and one was Latino. Our church sizes were about the same, so we had similar professional challenges which made our discussions productive from a professional point of view.

When we first came together, our discussions started out on a surface level. But as we came to know one other, our talk became more honest and our trust became deeper. We started sharing some of our personal, emotional, and deeply held secrets and failures. As one would share, so would another and coping strategies would emerge and be presented. It wasn't long before we trusted each other enough to challenge, admonish, and exhort one another. But it was never received as threatening to our egos or self-esteems because the trust factor had become so deep and apparent between us. Over time, transparency, disclosure, and honesty concerning how we felt about each other's abilities, marriages, and ministries was shared freely.

It was the most healing, uplifting, beneficial, and beautiful time of my ministry; and it was that for all three of us. Yes, we were busy. But we made time, sometimes a whole day to get together and share because it was so encouraging to be with one another.

Did it make our churches grow? Not necessarily. Did it balance out our schedules so we had more time? No. It actually became tougher and tougher to find time to come together because we would want to put more and more time into our gatherings—time none of us had. But it caused each of us to understand at an experiential level the value of exhorting and admonishing one another.

A name given to this type of group in today's Christian vernacular is *accountability groups.*

I have found that in the church you don't just set out to have fully functioning accountability groups. As I said before, the baggage some of our most functional people carry around with them these days combines with the normal pride and mistrust levels in each of us to make effective accountability groups a definite challenge. But at all costs it needs to happen—even more today than ever before. The amount of beauty in the church of Jesus Christ that is being missed in people's lives because they aren't a part of groups like these is heartbreaking to me personally; and I believe it is the same for the Master. The positive implications of successful groups like these, when considering and compared to the alternative, is staggering. Without them we are prideful, hard-hearted, untrusting, low in self-esteem, resistant to change, calloused, and clammed-up Christians; and oh yes, we are prone to falling.

With them we can become genuine, transparent, sound, stable, pliable, tender, and more victorious Christians.

Pastors and leaders need to bite the bullet and run to this type of relational environment in order to bring wholeness to their lives and ministries, and to set an example for their people to follow. Lay persons who have pastors not engaged in this kind of relational and spiritual obedience to God's Word should do it to set an example for their pastors.

EDIFICATION

In Romans 4:19 Paul instructs believers to edify one another. I'm sure I don't need to give extensive explanation concerning the concept of edification. It simply means to build up. An edifice is a building. If we edify a person, we build that one up emotionally, mentally, and spiritually.

To help us understand more accurately, all we need do is look at its opposite—to tear down.

We have plenty of tearing down going on among Christians, don't we? People tear down the worship leader, the assistant pastor, the Sunday school superintendent, the church secretary, the small group leader, the youth leader, the children's church leader, and the pastor—all in the name of concern for the ministry. People tear down Aunt Ethel, Cousin Billy, Brother Sam, Uncle Fred, and Aunt Harriet. People tear down their friends, their fellow employees, their neighbors, their bosses, and their enemies. People tear down their country, their government, their congressional leaders, their political party, and their city officials.

If tearing down were a fatal disease, very few of us would be alive.

People who tear down people tear apart relational harmony in their neighborhoods, their work places, their

168

families, their schools, their clubs, and their churches. Sometimes they purpose to do so. But usually they are just emotionally out of control.

The sources of tearing down are low self-esteem, anger, hatred, jealousy, poor upbringing, poor models, and a troubled psyche. A person may possess all, some, or only one of these and be just as destructive. Often those who tear down get their criticisms confused with constructive criticism. They justify their tearing down by calling their destructive criticism constructive. But the anger involved, the intent to hurt, and the looming outcome of discord in the ranks are the telltale signs that the clear motivation was to tear down.

I'm sure you have been in the presence of one who tears down. It's debilitating, discouraging, and grievous.

For those who are inclined to dividing with criticism, it gives them a temporary and false sense of satisfaction, much like a drug or alcohol will cause one to forget their troubles. People can actually become addicted to the encouragement boost a put-down can lend momentarily to their self-esteem. But it is a false and short-lived feeling of encouragement. It does not bring a lasting increase to their self-esteem. Instead it creates an even greater self-esteem deficit. That is why they tear someone else down again as soon as they get another opportunity. They do it for the temporary fix.

Proverbs 6:16–19 says, "These six things the Lord hates, yes, seven are an abomination to Him: A proud look, A lying tongue, Hands that shed innocent blood, A heart that devises wicked plans, Feet that are swift in running to evil, A false witness who speaks lies, And one who sows discord among brethren."

I have a theory. The reason Solomon capped this list with the one he did is because it is the one God hates the most. My theory continues. The reason God hates it the most is because it was the strategy Lucifer used to incite the rebellion that occurred in heaven among the angels. The result was: one third of the angelic host fell, were cast out of heaven, and became the demonic host under their leader and the instigator, the former angel of light—now Satan. (See Revelation 12:9.) He was the first to sow discord, and with it tore apart the very structure and harmony in heaven. And he has used the strategy in churches and other faith-organizations quite effectively ever since.

I realize some speculation surrounds my theory, but can you see the truth in it? The poetic style Solomon uses is one designed to build momentum until he makes his final and intended point—the one that propagates dissention among His people is hated by God. This is the only place in the Bible where God's hatred is actually aimed at an individual rather than a sin or a practice, suggesting the only type of person God hates is one who sows discord among His children—or one who tears down. It's just my theory.

That is not to say their sin is unpardonable. But it is certainly detestable to God.

Contrast all of that with the person who edifies—who builds up other people and the church. At the very least, it represents a heart that brings joy to the heart of God.

My remembrance goes back to when Israel was in the wilderness. Moses had just sent twelve men into the Promised Land to spy it out. (See Numbers 14:1–10.) Ten came back with an evil report. The other two (Joshua and Caleb) tore their clothes and pleaded with the people to not listen to the evil report of the other ten. They tried to reverse the tearing down of faith that the ten faithless men had begun. Not only did they fail, but the congregation tried to stone Joshua and Caleb for their attempt to maintain unity.

Every Israelite present in the congregation that day died before Israel crossed over the Jordan River into Canaan, except Joshua and Caleb. And that included Moses and Aaron. The two edifiers—the two men who tried to build up and encourage, among the two and a half million people that fateful day of the evil report—were the only ones allowed to enter the Promised Land. Furthermore, they were allowed to live through the conquest of Canaan and were granted God's favor to possess their inheritance along with the generation that replaced their doubting parents.

God loves encouragers. He loves and blesses edifiers. He wants as many edifiers in His church as He can find. Beautiful is the environment surrounding a person or a church that seeks no opportunity to tear down. They only seek to build up.

PRAY FOR ONE ANOTHER

Outside of a romantic relationship, when was the last time someone at your work called you and said, "I thought of you all day long the other day? You came to my mind, and I took it as an epiphany to bathe you in my thoughts. I thought you may have been in trouble, stressed, scared, or tempted to do something rash, so I cradled you in my concerns in an effort to protect you from a possible calamity. I woke up from my dreams with you on my mind, so I embraced you with my most earnest heart hug with the intent—if possible—to shelter you, in case danger was lurking at your life's door."

Outside of this sounding a little bit strange, when was the last time someone who didn't know God cared about you in this manner? It's my guess that the answer is: Never!

Have you ever thought about what hell is like? Some hard-drinking unbelievers think hell is going to be one big bash. They think, or hope, that when their wild and woolly lifestyle lands them in hell—they will rendezvous with their past buddies and yuck it up, drink it up, and high-five it up for all eternity with them. And they will do it with hell's flames being no more scorching than the heat of the spicy salsa they might consume at their post-earth party. It is one of the grand denials perpetrated by the great deceiver.

The Bible rather teaches, once a life wakes up in hell following a person's death, that person will instantly retreat into a self-absorbed state of physical and emotional pain so great and so spiritually and regionally distant from others that there will be no opportunity or desire to *party down* with friends. Eternal resentment will more likely be the emotion that will prevail toward friends, if there were a chance to connect with those friends at all. It will no doubt be this way because a person in hell will only be able to mentally digest the regrets of their choice to not choose Christ during his or her life; because deep within they will know that they alone rejected the Savior. No, self-blame will characterize hell—eternal, self-absorbed focus on one's own physical, mental, and emotional foolishness and pain for not responding to Christ in his or her life, in an environment of unfathomable torment. No, there will be no partying with others in hell.

Why all this depressing hell-talk?

In this life people are also extremely self-absorbed with pain and individual crises. Consequently, concern for others is more often than not thousands of miles away from people's consciences. The point is, people are in pain. And even in their best deeds, they are filled with self-righteous and self-focused coping strategies in an effort to feel better about their lives and their eternal destinies.

I say all this to help you see that—across the board—people are very focused on themselves. It is part of the sin nature. It started when Eve began to believe Satan's lie that she could be somebody; specifically, she could be like God. Once she sold the lie to her husband, the sin of self-absorption became the trademark branded on humanity and the ever-widening disease that characterizes the depravity of the human condition.

And it is ugly!

We see it every day.

I see it in my own heart and at times I want to scream in disgust and pain because of the grief my self-focused tendencies cause me. I hate how I look when I gaze at myself in the mirror and see someone so enamored with himself that he easily allows the concerns of people to fall from him as easily as water rolls off a duck's back—out of sight, out of mind.

But God did something to form an attitude in His people that would be completely unlike depraved humanity. He gave a salvation to man that would be so influenced by His Spirit, and so filled with His love, and so unlike the depravity around him that it would have the potential to shed the selfish tendencies of his depraved condition so that he could genuinely and selflessly care for the concerns of others.

Miraculously, when one turns his life over to Christ and is born of the Spirit, there emerge two green sprouts out of that person's new birth: love for God and love for His followers. Then, as their love for one another grows, one of the budding flowers of their love for other believers is a desire to pray for them.

Over the course of my ministry, I can't count the number of times a Christian friend, ministry colleague, or a believer in our church would tell me, "I was thinking about you the other day and the Lord prompted me to pray for you." Or, "God woke me up last night with you on my heart. So I brought you before the Lord in prayer." Or, "last week I was driving to work and you flashed across my mind. I felt like it was a commission from the Lord to pray for you. So I did. Is everything all right?"

In what walk of life other than Christianity do you find this kind of love, care, and intimacy? None that I know of.

Our love for God stimulates our love for one another, and the whole package sparks the practice of prayer to God for our newfound spiritual family members.

This thing called praying for one another is unprecedented in our world because no human practice holds all the elements necessary to produce this kind of concern for others.

All of this is to say nothing about the fact that the power of believing prayer has the miraculous ability to summon the power of God for those we pray for. And when that happens, which is often, the camaraderie between Christian brothers and sisters is enhanced even more.

When Christians, male or female, are praying to God for one another, the relational bond between them becomes stronger and stronger. Regardless of whether or not they see an immediate miraculous response from God's power, there is a miraculous cementing of love and support between them.

And you guessed it, it is beautiful.

People (especially men) are afraid of intimacy. It leaves them too vulnerable, too weak, too exposed. But prayer to God for others breaks down those fears and cultivates a beautiful environment of oneness in the lives of those who call themselves followers of Christ.

FELLOWSHIP WITH ONE ANOTHER

My wife has a huge family. She has two brothers and two sisters along with their spouses and children and her mother. All together, along with our children, the family could make up a small church. Recently we moved back home after thirty-five years of ministry travels. It seems any small excuse will bring the whole family together after church for a Sunday dinner. When that happens, wow! The amount of noise, laughter, fun, and food is incredible. We're all Christians. We all love God. We are all from similar religious persuasions and theologies, so arguments don't ensue. We are all human so our gatherings aren't impervious to disagreements and occasional hurt feelings. But by and large, our times together are pretty darn good.

But it is not so with other kinds of human gatherings.

Families without Christian faith to unite them may have similar dinner gatherings and parties, family reunions, and immediate family get-togethers where good times are experienced. But without the common denominator of Christ's love to unite them, many of those gatherings are strained with criticism, unforgiveness, bitterness, drunkenness, and the like. Over the years I have been invited to enough of these types of gatherings—or become privy to the goings-on that take place at some of them—that I am well aware of the dynamics that occur when these kinds of families come together.

Then there are office and work-related gatherings that are filled with backbiting, criticism, jockeying for position and attention, drunken foolhardiness, and gossip.

There are town dances and hullabaloos that bring people together for special events.

There are impromptu parties after softball games or high school football games at local pubs.

There are dinner parties, frat parties, holiday parties, wedding parties, anniversary parties, and any-excuse-to-get-together parties.

All of these latter kinds of gatherings look like Christian fellowship, but they lack two things: the Christian and the fellowship.

Some of these events may have Christians in attendance. And the Christians there may be very involved in Christian activities while there, like being a witness or praying for their lost friends. But there is clearly no Christian flavor to their event. Someone may haphazardly use the term fellowship to describe their gathering. But the term *fellowship* as it was used to describe what the early Christians did in the Bible cannot be duplicated in any other kind of gathering. It could only be experienced in get-togethers designed for Christians.

When someone is mightily redeemed by Christ's blood; and that person's life is powerfully transformed by the Spirit of God who now dwells within that one; and he or she deeply loves and appreciates God for His grace to accept that one into His family and bring that individual from death unto life, it is a beautiful miracle. It is the most wondrous and astounding phenomenon in all of life.

It all describes what goes into the making of a genuine Christian. (See 2 Corinthians 5:17.)

When another person who has had the same life-changing experience comes together with another of like experience in a setting that lends itself to mutual appreciation for the God who has done this miracle for both of them, it doubles the beauty and the wonder.

When several people gather together who share this common bond in an environment that has been facilitated for the purpose of enjoying God's miracle in them and enjoying each other, the beauty and wonder is almost too glorious to describe. That is Christian fellowship.

Yes, the Christians described above are flawed. And yes, their humanity can get in the way of the beauty sometimes. But the beauty of Christ's church can always outshine these disruptions in an environment where true Christian fellowship takes place.

Now don't confuse this environment with gatherings of some Christians who enjoy each other's company but seem to have misplaced their deep appreciation for God somewhere along the line, as well as awareness of His presence in and among them as they come together. These gatherings cannot really be labeled true Christian fellowship. Christians getting together can be just Christians getting together, and have nothing to do with Christian fellowship.

But when Christians come together in an environment that is fun-loving, filled with love, absent of dissention; marked by unity, awareness of, and appreciation for God's presence, that is true Christian fellowship. And when it is occurring, a beauty is present that all can discern. Some unbelieving people don't understand it. Others may not believe it, but they can detect its beauty.

In the first church where I was pastor, we began having what we referred to as hootenannies. They were held on a Sunday night once a year in the fall. They were designed to *just be fun*. We laughed, we sang, we presented skits, we told testimonies, we ate food, we shouted, and had so much fun some thought it must be sinful.

Some of our people invited some of their friends, who weren't Christians, to one of these gatherings. At one point just after they arrived, I saw these friends standing off to the side looking strangely at the antics of our hootenanny, and I decided to wander over and assess the situation. I asked their names, and they answered and told me who had invited them. Then I asked them if they were OK because they looked a bit bewildered as they were watching us.

The man glanced over at his female friend and said, "Well...actually...no, we're not OK."

I said, "Then...can I help you in any way?"

He cleared his throat and answered, "Yes...um...you can tell us.... What's the catch?"

"Excuse me!" I said with my own degree of confusion.

The man said, "Well...people seem to be having fun. They're telling jokes. They are slapping each other on the back. No one's drinking and no one is taking drugs—at least it doesn't look like it. They aren't cussing or fighting or telling dirty stories or pouting in the corner. And they're doing it all in church. And I just wondered—what is really going on? Are you paying them to act like this? When the party is over will they go back to their miserable selves? What's the catch?"

I didn't know what to say. Finally after I regained equilibrium I said, "There isn't any catch that I know of. We just love God, and we love each other. It's called Christian fellowship. Why don't you sit down and join us?"

They did. They started attending church and in time became Christians and started getting in on the fun.

Some people look suspiciously at genuine Christian fellowship because knowing human nature the way they do, they don't believe it could be authentic. There must be a catch. That many people couldn't possibly love each other that much. There have to be a lot of phonies in the crowd. There has to be some gossip, some backbiting, some jealousy, some criticism going on.

Genuine Christian fellowship doesn't just happen at hullabaloos. It happens in small groups that are saturated with Christ's love and dominated by Christians loving each other in that environment. It happens at gatherings of Christians where pretense and pride are absent, having been squeezed out by the overpowering presence of God's love and people's endearments to one another in His name. It happens where Jesus is glorified, where people are loved, and where there is no room for hatred.

Where true Christian fellowship is, there is beauty.

And so it is with every one of the "one anothers." I could talk about how each one—when done the way God intended—would bring another aspect of His loving beauty into His church. But I don't think I need to. I think you get my drift.

Part III

❧ *Behaviors of Little Ones* ❧

At that time the disciples came to Jesus, saying, 'Who then is greatest in the kingdom of heaven?' Then Jesus called a little child to Him, set him in the midst of them, and said, "Assuredly, I say to you, unless you are converted and become as little children, you will by no means enter the kingdom of heaven. Therefore whoever humbles himself as this little child is the greatest in the kingdom of heaven. Whoever receives one little child like this in My name receives Me. Whoever causes one of these little ones who believe in Me to sin, it would be better for him if a millstone were hung around his neck, and he were drowned in the depth of the sea."

—Matthew 18:1–6

Then they brought little children to Him, that He might touch them; but the disciples rebuked those who brought them. But when Jesus saw it, He was greatly displeased and said to them, "Let the little children come to Me, and do not forbid them; for such is the kingdom of God. Assuredly, I say to you, whoever does not receive the kingdom of God as a little child will by no means enter it." And He took them up in His arms, laid His hands on them, and blessed them.

—Mark 10:13–16

In each of the first three gospels (Luke's description can be found in Luke 18:15–17 and repeats Mark's account above) the writers made it a point to emphasize how Jesus felt about children. Jesus didn't just like kids, He saw them as models for us to follow. And He knew enough about kids to attribute to them some pretty enlightening character qualities.

First He says (my paraphrase), "The whole kingdom of heaven emanates the kind of attitude and heart that little children have." Then he goes a step farther and says, "If any of you try to enter the kingdom with an attitude that is different than that of a little child, you won't get in—period!" Then Jesus says, "Whoever humbles himself as a little child, that person is greatest in the kingdom of heaven."

The gospel writers were noticeably moved by this perspective of Jesus. Jesus loved kids, and yes, He protected them. But mostly He admired them. He knew there was something in the hearts of little children that must be present in the hearts of His followers in order for them to be His genuine followers. They were His model for kingdom behavior.

Recently, as a kind of sabbatical, I took a job teaching sports classes and clinics for children at the YMCA. While working there, I also refereed basketball and soccer games. In addition during this time, I substitute taught for the public school system. This gave me an upfront view of kids.

At the time, I wondered why I had ended up doing this kind of work. In hindsight, I think I know why. First, I love kids and enjoy working with them, so it was a refreshing time for me. But it also gave me an opportunity to observe kids at a level that enabled me to catch a glimpse of what makes children so special in the eyes of Jesus. There are some things remarkably and uniquely beautiful about the hearts of little children that can become traits to model for Christian adults and gatherings of Christ's church.

Please open your hearts as I talk to you about the beautiful behaviors of children and how God wants us to be like them.

Chapter 13

⁓

The Power of the High Five

JUST ABOUT EVERY kid I know is powerless to resist slapping someone's hand when it is held up in front of them in high five pose. Try it sometime. I dare you to test my theory. Hold your hand up in front of a kid, especially ten years old or younger, and act like you are requesting some skin. Nine times out of ten that youngster will respond in like manner and will usually have a smile on his or her face.

I don't know when the high five began. Some sources offer a few suggestions, but no one knows for sure. It must have been when the traditional handshake lost its luster. But kids jumped on it. Parents even began to teach their kids to do the high five before they took their first step or said their first word. It has become a universal communication device for children. For a kid it says: the person in front of me is interested in me and I am interested in that person. The child's accompanying smile says: this person is speaking my language and might be able to relate to me. It screams: though I may not be able to decipher their thoughts at this point in my young life, the person extending his hand for me to slap cares about me.

When I was teaching kids' sports classes for the YMCA, I used the high five to control the behavior, win the trust, and capture the hearts of the four- and five-year-olds I was teaching. When they came running into the gym for the class, usually well out in front of their parents who were trying to keep up, they would literally come shouting, "Chriiiiiis!" with their hands up almost demanding a high five fix. They hadn't been in class for a week, and they needed to speak the high five language again.

We always began the baseball, soccer, or basketball class with stretching exercises, followed by running to warm up their tiny bodies and teach them how to begin every workout.

The running was a high five extravaganza.

I would line the little tykes up on the basketball court end line. There were usually anywhere from ten to twenty kids, depending on how many had signed up for the class.

I would first stand on the foul line, and when I said, "On your mark! Get set! Go!" the little lads and lasses would run to me, converge on me, and slap me a high five. And as they ran in a beeline for my position on the foul line, the smiles on their faces would stretch from ear to ear. Then they would return to the starting line as fast as they could.

Then I would move to the half-court line and repeat the launch sequence. "On your mark! Get set! Gophers!" And there would be several false starts because they were only allowed to go when I said, "Go!" And I could be very clever, so they had to listen carefully. After the false starts, they were instructed to, "Quick... get back on the line because Coach Chris can be very tricky." Then I would say, "On your mark! Get set! Googlie eyes! Goggles! Gingerbread man! Golf balls! Go!" They would run as fast as their little legs could carry them with their hands ready to slap mine. After our palms made contact, they would run back to the end line where they came from and line up preparing to do it all again.

I would then move to the three-quarter court line, and we would all do the same thing another time.

Last, I would place myself at the opposite end of the gym under the basket. The kids all knew what was going to happen next because we did it every class—over and over again. I would go through the same routine, and they would go through their series of false starts until they heard clearly, "Go!" Then they would run at me in an all-out sprint. As they approached my position at the end line, at the last second I would slide one way or the other and begin running backwards in circles around the gym with my hands extended teasing them to catch up with me and slap mine. But I would be just ahead of them and just out of their reach until finally, after several circles, I would let them catch me. And in chorus, they would scream and slap my extended hand in victory. Sometimes I would fall to the floor with my hands stretched out, and they would, in predictable response, doggie pile on top of me slapping my hand and screaming at the top of their lungs as they fell—all while their parents watched from the bleachers in joyful disbelief. It was a high five extravaganza.

Whenever I would sit the kids down with crossed legs in a powwow session to discuss the rules of the sport they were learning, the high five was my celebratory response to a correct answer.

I would say, "Who can tell me something about basketball?" They would all raise their hands, and when I pointed at one of them, he or she would say dribbling; another would say passing; another, shooting, defense, lay-up, pivot, or some other aspect of basketball we had taught them. And when they said it, a high five would be the reward, the affirmation, the celebration, and the relational stimulus between us.

In fact, after every good, bad, or ugly performance of a fundamental action—like throwing in baseball, kicking in soccer, or passing in basketball—a high five would follow from me or one of the staff assisting me.

The kids ate it up.

But think with me. What does the high five really mean?

It means much more than a handshake, even to adults. The next time your team wins a game, try expressing your emotion with a handshake. It just doesn't cut it!

When my team scores a touchdown and a fellow fan slaps my hand about head height, it is a celebration of a good result. But it is so much more. It is an expression of unity. It is a declaration of camaraderie. It is an outcry of joy. It is a statement that life isn't all that serious. It is fun. It is laughter. It is excitement. It is victory. It is affirmation. It is confirmation. It is information. It is exhilaration. It is life. And yet it is an expression that seriously and with conviction declares what is important to us.

And that's just for adults.

For kids the joy and importance of the high five is multiplied ten fold.

When the same exhilaration that the high five gives to kids is in the church, it is beautiful, stimulating, attractive and rejuvenating all at the same time.

These kinds of words fill the Bible in an effort to describe the Christian experience among believers: celebration, victory, joy, love, encouragement, edification, exultation, laughter, uplifting, accepting, fellowship, unity, and cherishing.

And yet, it is words like pious, mourn, tradition, discipline, seriousness, judgementalism, and legalism that wind up shaping the posture and expression of many of our Christian and church environments.

What posture describes your Christian and church environment, head down or head up? Psalms 3:3 says, "But You, O Lord, are a shield for me, My glory and the One who lifts up my head." While a life without God, or at least a life absent of His hope, is described in Psalms 43:5, "Why are you downcast, O my soul? Why so disturbed within me? Put your hope in God" (NIV).

I see the Christian life as an *up* experience, not a down one.

When Israel sinned in the wilderness, as a punishment from God for their poor behavior, they were attacked by poisonous snakes. In His mercy, God told Moses to have a bronze image of a snake placed on a pole erected high in the center of the camp. When the people who had been bitten looked up at the serpentine figure, they would be healed. Most theologians feel that through this, God was making a statement that their deliverance and hope would always depend on the people posturing their heads and hearts to look up, or figuratively, look to Him.

In the gospel of John, Jesus clarified the meaning when He said, "As Moses lifted up the serpent in the wilderness, even so must the Son of Man be lifted up" (John 3:14). "And I, if I am lifted up from the earth, will draw all peoples to myself" (John 12:32). All together, the One we look up to as Savior and Deliverer and the One who has won our victory on the cross is Jesus. But to not look up to Him is to look down in defeat in every walk of life.

Correct me if I am wrong, but isn't the high five an expression that is *up* as opposed to down? And I refuse to offer a disclaimer for what some might feel is an exaggeration of the analogy.

I think Christians and churches alike need to adopt the language of the kid's high five, all without eliminating any of the emotions it represents. A similar enthusiasm was what the early church was about in the first chapters of Acts. It is what it should be today. And it is what the church needs to be if it is going to reach the culture we live in.

All around us is a culture that is oppressed with dysfunction in families and our society, more psychotic behavior than ever before, characterized by depression, ADD, bipolar disorders, and the like. Then there are wars, threats of nuclear armament, global warming, the depletion of the ozone layer, terrorist invasion, super volcanoes, earthquakes, tsunamis, and poverty. And that is the short list.

This is not a pep talk on talking positive, keeping your chin up, not living in the gutter, or being a person of faith by staying on the sunny side of life.

This is a challenge for churches and Christians to radiate the high five spirit Christ has inserted into every believer, and the high five environment He has intended to be in His church. Not for any other reason except that it is a much more biblical, uplifting, encouraging, and beautiful environment to exist in than the oppressive, legalistic, depressing, and frankly discouraging auras that surround many Christians and churches today.

Have you ever tried to talk to a little tot about the depressing and overwhelming troubles of your life? If you haven't, that is good; you shouldn't. They wouldn't be able to understand you anyway. They would look at you with their mouths wide open, in utter boredom and incomprehension because they wouldn't have the slightest clue what you are talking about. They might even start to cry because they think you are trying to hurt them.

But throw up a hand in front of them requesting a little elevated skin, and they will wipe their tears, sniffle a few times, and a smile will form on their faces as they celebrate with you—even if they don't know why they are celebrating.

Kids understand celebration. But they don't understand the depressing side of life. Maybe it's because they have yet to experience it. Or, maybe it's because God wants kids to be an example to us to keep celebration at the forefront of our hearts, lives, families, churches, and testimonies. If God is the great, all-powerful and all-loving One the Bible describes, shouldn't we be filled with hope and trust rather than discouragement and despair—even as we look at the troubles in our lives?

When my kids were little, after an activity at church or school, we would ask, "Did you have fun?" Their response would usually be, "Boy did I!" As they grew older we would still ask the same question, even in college. But at a certain point we stopped asking it that way. Instead we would ask, "Did you have a good time?" Or, "Did you enjoy yourself?" We avoided the word fun, as if fun was exclusively an emotion affecting children and a word solely assigned to describe something kids should experience. Looking back, the change in the way I asked this question of my kids as they grew older almost seemed like what the disciples may have been thinking when they rebuked parents for bringing their children to Jesus. Kids do childish things and have fun. Adults are about important things—serious things. Fun is not something adults should have—a good time, yes, an enjoyable time, perhaps, but not fun.

In His statement in Mark 10:14, "Let the little children come to Me, and do not forbid them; for such is the kingdom of God," I believe Jesus is giving adults permission to have fun—even in church. Or maybe a better way to say it is, especially in church. After all, if kids are all about fun, and we are supposed to be like them, shouldn't our hearts and the environment where we gather be filled with fun?

A high five spirit is not a denial of reality. It is not a sweeping of the emotional pain in our lives under the proverbial carpet. It is not an ignoring of the serious side of relationship with Jesus. It is a revival of the expectant and celebrative part of Christianity that must be present if we are to experience the fullness of joy that God intends for relationship with Him to have.

I have a certain kind of relationship with all the kids in my church. You guessed it—it's marked by the high five. When I am standing in a doorway and one or several walk through it, I through up one of my hands and they respond in like manner slapping my palm as they go by. It's almost robotic. If I didn't see a snicker or an outright smile on their faces as they passed, I would think they were electronically programmed to respond.

Sometimes when I see a kid in the foyer, I will play a game with him or her that I call "slap the moving high five." You know, I will hold out my hand and when he goes to hit it, I'll move it to make him miss. Then I have a captive child. That little one is challenged—no, compelled—to make contact with my hand.

Not long ago I had two nine-year-olds totally engaged. They were trying desperately to hit my hand. But I was especially elusive. Then I put my hand in front of one of the boys' faces for the other to hit. As if there were a force guiding him, the other went for it. Realizing he was about to pound his friend in the face if I moved my hand, he stopped about an inch short, and he and his friend began to giggle and laugh so hard, they almost fell to the floor. Honestly, I was laughing as hard as they were.

There is a seven-year-old girl in our church named Jamie. She is the daughter of one of our staff members and I have a high five relationship with her as well. Just about every time I see her, I throw up my hand and she runs over to me, jumps as high as her little legs will catapult her, and she slaps my hand as hard as she can with a glowing smile on her face stretching from ear to ear. I won't let her walk by me without giving me a hand slap. If she tries, even in fun, I'll say, "Hey—Jamie! Get back here!" And she will turn around with a smile on her face capable of lighting up a dark room, she will take about three leaping bounds in my direction, jump as high as she can, and put a mean smack on my hand.

The other day Jamie walked by my office door with her coat and backpack on. She glanced in my direction with a smirk on her face as she passed. I knew what she wanted. I got up and walked quickly to my door. Though she was walking away from me and was covered with a bulky jacket and cumbersome backpack, I could see her whole body shaking as she walked. I knew she was giggling—just waiting for me to come to my door to scold her for not giving me a high five.

I said, "Hey!"

Anticipating exactly what I wanted, she spun around on cue and ran for me. She was donning a smile from one side of her face to the other. Her beautiful curly blonde locks were bouncing all around her face and her grin as she jumped for my extended hand and whacked it. However, it seemed as if she did so not with her hand, but with the joyful and burden-free glee of her heart.

Then she simply turned and walked out of the room. As she did, a tear came to my eye as I pondered the innocence of tiny lives.

As I turned to go back to my desk, I thought, "How beautiful believers and churches would be if such a heart as Jamie's—and every other child's in the world—could exist, if only in simple expression, in the Christian environment. What would it be like if the celebrative, loving, happy, gleeful posture of a child—as seen in the simple slap of a hand—could be present in the environment of a church; certainly not ignoring the serious or grave concerns that may arise or exist? But what would happen if at least a significant element of a child's heart as seen in the simple act of an elevated hand slap could be prevalent in the hearts of Christians across our land?"

My thought was simply, "How beautiful!"

Who wouldn't want to be surrounded by an environment like that? Who wouldn't want to spend the remainder of their experience before the Lord returns around an environment that contains the kind of innocence, happiness, peace, and sense of safety that surrounds the heart of a child? It seems to me that it would be reminiscent of the environment that characterized the Garden of Eden before the fall. Then at the end of time we would be translated to heaven. Who wouldn't want that?

How would one begin to form that kind of atmosphere in a church? I'm not completely sure. But I think it needs to start with the one reading these words. Start spending time around, learning from, and appreciating little children. Discover the part of their hearts Jesus would like to see in His "big kids." Then ask God to sprout, nurture, and blossom that heart in you, and then your church.

Chapter 14

╶╮

Kids Believe

ENDRIX WAS FOUR years old. His parents named him after the famous guitarist Jimi Hendrix. His father was a musician and greatly admired the music idol so much he named his first son after the famous rock star.

Hendrix had natural talent athletically, but he had a problem. He believed. He believed so completely, he had trouble separating fact from fiction and pretend from reality.

The dreaded pretend activity was the dribbling game called "What Time Is It, Mr. Fox"? Hendrix thought it was real. Try as we did to convince him that it was only a game, and that I, Coach Chris, was not a fox, when the game was in full swing he couldn't believe it.

Here is how the game worked. Each four or five year old would line up on the end line of the basketball court with a tiny kid-sized basketball. As Mr. Fox, I would go to the mid-court line. In unison the kids would shout to me, "What time is it, Mr. Fox?" In response, with a sinister look and a playful snarl on my lips, I would rub my hands together and say, "It's five o'clock." The tykes would then walk toward me and count out five dribbles as they bounced their balls. In a perfect world, they would all catch their balls on the fifth dribble, come to a stop, and still be in a straight line. But usually half of the fifteen or so kids dribbled their basketballs on their feet or knees or missed hitting them with their hands, and the balls would scatter, bouncing or rolling across the gym floor. Then they would chase their errant basketballs, grab them, run back to the approximate place where they lost control, and come to a stop holding their pint-sized ball. Hopefully, as the weeks went on, their dribbling would improve—but not always. When all the kids were back in position again, they would repeat together in chorus, "What time is it, Mr. Fox?" My response may have been, "It's nine o'clock." And they would all begin the count, walk, and errant dribble routine again.

Because they were getting closer to me, I would continue to back up until my back was against the opposite wall from where the activity began. After each dribbling segment, and after they had gotten back in place, they would repeat their question to me all together again, to which I would respond; it's two o'clock, it's four o'clock, or it's one o'clock. Until finally, when the little ones had gotten very close to me, I would utter the highly anticipated and dreaded words, "It's dinnertime!" At which, the kids all screamed, turned, and headed back to their starting point, clutching their balls and running for dear life with me, or should I say Mr. Fox, in close pursuit. The slowest one was caught by Mr. Fox, and playfully grabbed up and then gobbled up (pretend-style).

Hendrix was the slowest the first time he played the game, so he was caught. When I caught him and held him in my arms as I ran, his tiny eyes looked up at me in horror. His mouth was open as though ready to scream, and as I dropped my head into his tummy and faked a gobbling sound, Hendrix began to wail in mortal terror. A bit frightened myself, I stopped up short and brought him over to his mother who was sitting on the bleachers watching.

She said, "Hendrix, it's just pretend. Coach Chris isn't really a fox. He is just pretending to be a fox. It's part of the game."

But from that point on, in each class Hendrix took part in, we couldn't convince him to give the game a try. He would go over to his mother on the bleachers and curl up next to her whenever we played the game. About the fourth class we decided to forgo the game because it was just too hard on Hendrix.

Kids believe.

When my first son was six years old, as analytical as he was even then, he still believed in Santa—but he was having doubts. That Christmas Eve we had a discussion about how Santa might get into our house since we didn't have a chimney. The lies we told him that night were serious transgressions which we would consider repenting of for years. But the result for my son was a tentative acceptance of the concept of Santa, at least for that holiday season.

As soon as our son went to bed, to bring further credence to the deception, my wife and I went to work putting the presents under the tree.

The next morning I awoke first and checked my son to be sure he was still asleep. He was, but I closely monitored his waking for the next hour so I could time my final act of deceit. As he began to stir, from my bed in a deep voice,

I uttered the words every kid longs to hear somewhere between Christmas Eve and Christmas morning.

"Ho...ho...ho! Merry Christmas, everybody! Merry Christmas!" Then I rolled over and pretended to be asleep.

A few moments later my son was standing over me and shaking me. I acted as though I had been asleep, and said in a groggy voice, "What is it, Jeff?"

"Dad...that was you, wasn't it?" he asked.

"What do you mean?" I responded in a sleepy voice.

"That was you that just said Merry Christmas...wasn't it, Dad?" he insisted.

"I didn't hear anything, Jeff. You just woke me up. Why, did you hear Santa?" The lies were flowing freely from my lips as though I had no conscience at all.

"Are you sure you didn't say that, Dad?"

"No," I lied. "It must have really been Santa. Did you check to see if there were any presents under the tree?"

My son's eyes widened, and he pranced as briskly as his little and still sleepy legs would take him into the room where our Christmas tree was standing.

Before I could pull myself out from under the covers, Jeff shouted excitedly from the other room, "He came dad, Santa really came. Look at all the presents."

That was the last year we could pull the wool over his eyes on what has come to be known among us Schimels as *The Santa Claus Incident*. And there has been a standing controversy in our family ever since, as to whether or not Jeff actually fell for the Santa myth that year.

Kids believe.

Unfortunately there are scores of other things they believe that are much more damaging to their tiny lives.

Two years later Jeff began to stutter. It was the oddest thing. He stuttered for several weeks before I decided it was a problem serious enough for me to look into. When I found out the possible causes I was horrified. I found out I was the cause. No, it wasn't because I lied to him about Santa.

The information I researched said that one of the causes of children stuttering was parents who are impatient with or uninterested in their child's attempts to communicate with them. Often, when kids try to talk with their parents, Mom, Dad, or both are inattentive and their child becomes nervous and uncertain and often begins to stutter in all of their communication.

I knew it was me. I knew it because prior to that, I had been very impatient listening to my son as he had attempted to tell me different things; a story, an explanation of what he was doing in school, or something he had seen on television.

Right then, just after I beat myself up for being such a lousy dad, I determined I would never treat my son, or for that matter any other child, that way again.

The next time my son had something to tell me, I dropped everything I was doing to listen to him. And I focused my full attention on him. I didn't act impatient with his stuttering or his tale, or roll my eyes when it didn't come out just right. I didn't get bored with the content of his information. I just listened intently.

The next time he had a story to tell me, I did the same thing. For the next several days, I made it a point to listen to Jeff no matter what he wanted to talk to me about. If he had as much as a sentence to share with me at the dinner table, I put my knife and fork down and paid close attention to him. If he wanted to talk to me when I was working,

I put my work down and gave him my undivided attention. If he interrupted me while I was talking to someone from the church I was leading, I excused myself from the conversation, knelt down, and listened to my son. If I was on the phone, I cut my call short and attended to my child. His stuttering began to improve immediately. And within two weeks it stopped entirely and has never returned.

Since that stuttering lesson, I determined to listen to my children whenever they had something to tell me. I even started helping other parents with their kids. If a parent was talking to me, and their child interrupted, I would say, "Go ahead. Talk to your son or daughter. I can wait."

My son believed. He believed in me. My carelessness with his tender trust in me almost hurt him irreparably.

Kids believe.

Kids believe in Santa Claus, the Easter Bunny, the Tooth Fairy, leprechauns, pots of gold at the end of the rainbow, alligators under their beds, the Boogie Man, Peter Pan, and unicorns. Kids believe.

Kids believe in God.

When I was six years old, my mother was hanging paper around town for folks to try to gain some extra income for our family. She would bring me with her because there was no babysitter to watch me. One day she brought me to a house that was just down the street from where we lived. No one else was home, and she was hanging paper in an upstairs bedroom.

As usual when Mom worked, I was bored and wandered around the house investigating. I discovered on a downstairs table a dish with several coins in it. I looked up the stairs to see if my mother was looking or coming. When

I saw neither was the case, I heisted a nickel from the dish and put it in my pocket.

That night, while watching *Leave it to Beaver* with my father, the phone rang. I didn't pay much attention until I heard my mother say, "It's missing? Are you sure?"

All of a sudden, recollection of my crime flooded back into my mind, and I began to breathe hard. Within a few moments she hung up the phone and was standing over me with her hands on her hips and a stern look on her face.

Looking directly at me with suspicion shooting at me from her eyes like daggers, she said to my father, "Fay, that was Mrs. Rexford. She said that there was a nickel missing from the change dish on her downstairs table."

Then, while still looking at me, she turned her words toward me and said, "Chris, do you know anything about that?"

I looked up at her with terror in my eyes and stuttered, "I…I…I." Then I began to cry.

I received the spanking of my life—at least up to that point. My mom made me go over to the Rexfords', sit down in shame in front of them, apologize, and give back the nickel.

I'll tell you what, I learned my lesson.

But something else happened. My mother quoted a scripture to me, and though I was only six, it was etched into my brain to be there forever and ever, amen. She said, "Chris, maybe this will teach you what the Bible says, 'Be sure, your sin will find you out'" (Num. 32:23).

I believed it. In fact I still believe it today the same as I did then. I believed even at six years old. I couldn't figure out how anyone could have found out that I had taken a measly nickel out of a dish filled with all kinds of change including several nickels. Any natural explanation I tried to apply, even as I increased in age and reasoning power, wouldn't diminish the truth of that scripture. I knew my mother hadn't seen. I knew no one else was present to watch me perform the heist. I knew I had reasoned when I took it, "How could they miss a nickel out of so much change?" Perhaps there was a natural explanation, but be assured, then I believed. And even now, I still believe.

It's living proof—kids believe in God.

But once kids begin to get older, smarter, more world-wise, more informed, more educated and more adult, they cease believing. The first to go is Santa, and the rest of the fairy tales follow in time. Unfortunately, the greatest truth and the soundest reality that exists in our world, which is God, is often considered not believable right along with the fairy tales.

The culprit of a growing kid's disbelief in fairy tales is truth. The culprit of a growing kid's disbelief in God is a lie. The bad news is; both are brought in by adulthood.

But let's go back to one of the reasons Jesus exalts childhood. And that is, kids believe. They just do. Something in the heart of a child causes them to simply, humbly, and emphatically believe.

There is a stage of Christianity that very much resembles the heart of a child. In this stage, it seems apparent it is God's intention to bring childlike belief back to His followers.

I'm sure you are familiar with all the *reborn* and *childlike* statements in the Bible. Jesus told Nicodemus in John 3:3, "Unless one is born again, he cannot see the kingdom of God." And in Matthew 18:3 He said, "Unless you are converted and become as little children, you will by no means enter the kingdom of heaven." Paul in Galatians 4:29

talks about people being "born according to the Spirit." In 1 Corinthians 3:1 he refers to "babes in Christ." Peter, in 1 Peter 1:23, affirms the concept when he says, "Having been born again, not of corruptible but incorruptible." And in 1 John the beloved disciple mentions being "born of God" seven times. (See 1 John 3:9; 4:7; 5:1, 4, 18.)

A new babe in Christ has childlike belief just as children do. It's the same, but different. But it is so miraculous and so universal for new Christians that it can only be attributed to God's hand and His plan.

And once again a *child* believes.

In the first church I led as pastor, a man with an interesting background came to Christ. He was a hard man. He had been in gangs, prison, deadly fights, had been present for gang murders, and on drugs.

He survived that time in his life, which is unusual for people of his background, and was by that time married and trying to make a go of a normal life. All of his sin caught up with him though and fell onto his shoulders—in the form of crippling, Holy Spirit-induced guilt and conviction. He was invited to a Christian concert during this time by someone who went to our church. He opened his heart to Christ at that concert. God's presence filled him so completely he turned his life over to Christ on the spot. He was born again by the Spirit of God, and one of the first things he did after his conversion was to go out and purchase a beautiful, black, leather bound Bible.

This man's wife, however, who had also gone to the concert with her husband, was not so moved. She had been a good girl her whole life and figured she was going to heaven because of her goodness. In fact, she was glad for the change that had taken place in her husband; after all, he needed it. She called it a change he was required to make—but not her.

One day, with his new Bible in hand, he tried to talk to his wife about her need to become born again as he was. But she refused to hear him. The discussion turned into a heated argument, and in a huff she walked out the front door as she said, "I don't want to have anything to do with your born-again or your church."

Her husband followed her to the door and as she opened the car door to get in and drive away, he threw his beautiful new Bible at her. She never saw it. It sailed over her head and the car as she got into the driver's seat, and landed in the neighbor's bushes.

As she drove off, her husband went back inside, plopped down on the couch, and started to pout in a fit of frustration. After a few minutes as he began to cool off, he started to feel bad about having lost his temper with his wife. He thought, "How foolish and immature of me to treat her like that. How am I ever going to be an example of Christ to her now?"

Just then he remembered, "Not only did I lose my temper; I threw my Bible at my wife." As this dawned on him, he hurried outside and over to his neighbor's front yard to retrieve his holy writ. But when he arrived, the Bible was nowhere to be found. He looked everywhere. He looked high and low, up and down, east and west, north and south. He looked in the bushes and under them. He knocked on his neighbor's front door and asked them if they had been in the front yard and found his Bible. He asked people walking by on the street if they had been by earlier and seen his holy book. He got a ladder out and looked on his neighbor's roof. He spent three hours checking every nook and cranny of his neighbor's house, their yard, the bushes, and around the trees. The Bible had vanished.

As he was concluding his search, the thought came to him that God had taken his Bible as a lesson to him for fighting with his wife about becoming a Christian and doing something so unholy as throwing it at her. He became convinced that God had taken his Bible from him because he had used it to try to hurt his wife.

That is when he called me because he wanted me, as his pastor, to come over to his house to pray for him so God wouldn't punish him further. I came over, and upon arriving, I spent some time looking for his Bible as well.

But he was right—the Bible was gone.

In my mind, I thought someone must have seen the very nice book and taken it. But this newly born-again Christian refused to buy a natural explanation. If someone had walked by and picked it up, he felt God sent them. If they didn't, God had raptured the book to heaven. Why did he feel this?

The man believed.

After my unproductive search, as I sat in his house with him, I chose to believe too. Not for any other reason but I could see believing—for this new believer—was what was turning his heart toward repentance and a desire to apologize to his wife for his poor behavior. His tender and sincere apology to his wife was so out of the ordinary, it helped her to see the real phenomenon of change in her husband and contributed to her eventually becoming born again as well.

Kids believe—natural and spiritual kids. That is why Jesus wants his followers to be like little children. Hebrews 11:6 says, "Without faith it is impossible to please Him, for he who comes to God must believe that He is, and that He is a rewarder of those who diligently seek Him."

I often think about my more sophisticated, practical, and mature Christian perspective to come to this family's house to provide a logical explanation for what happened to the Bible. Each time I go there in my thoughts I conclude, "I was wrong to think it and wrong to try to persuade the man of it." It was wrong because I could have supervened child-like belief. I could have shamed him in his tender faith and lured him away from the kind of belief in God that the Lord wanted, not only from him, but from me also. And I could have stood in the way of his wife also coming to the faith. I could have "grown him up" early and caused him to see how things really were in the Christian world. I could have ruined his faith.

We think kids are cute and sweet when they express simple trust in Kris Kringle, a tooth fairy, and the Easter bunny. We even think, "I wish they would never grow up"—but know they will. And when they do, along with their departure from childhood will be a departure from their belief in these childhood myths.

The same sweetness is in new-born believers who have recently opened their hearts to Christ. They are new babes. But we need to remember they are also little children who believe. And we can think them cute, but we shouldn't think them immature because they possess the kind of simple faith Jesus wants all of us who know Him to possess—all the time.

This same sweetness is also present in churches that have simple childlike faith dwelling in and among their members. I'm not talking about immature belief. I'm talking about childlike belief in God. Without it, the Bible says, "It is impossible to please [God]" (Heb. 11:6). So we're not just talking about a sweet atmosphere in believers and churches.

We're talking about the kind of belief any Christian—young or old, mature or immature—should have.

I might add, this kind of childlike faith also generates miracles—the kind of miracles that fill the hearts of people with excitement and assurance that God is alive and well on planet Earth. (See Mark 11:24.) In their quest to grow up spiritually, so many churches and Christians have left behind their belief in God's miracle power. They have more information about Him and more verses memorized, but they don't believe anymore. They have faith—but they don't really believe.

But God calls us His children, and God's kids believe.

One of the most beautiful Christian atmospheres I have ever been in is filled with mature Christians who don't feel they are mature. Their faith is solid. They don't feel they know that much or are that grown up in Christ. They don't flaunt their biblical knowledge, though they have much. Neither do they walk in arrogance concerning their faith in God. They are just God's kids growing, not acting as though they have already attained or have reached perfection. (See Philippians 4:12.) But they are always growing up in all things into Him who is the head, Christ. (See Ephesians 4:15.) They aren't children who are tossed to and fro and carried about by every wind of doctrine. (See Ephesians 4:14.) And they aren't babes in that they are carnal and allow envy, strife, and divisions to be among them. (See 1 Corinthians 3:1-3.) But they are pleasing to God in that they believe. (See Hebrews 11:6.) And they are God's children in that they received Him as a child and have been given the right to become children of God. (See John 1:12.) They are even the greatest in God's kingdom because they have humbled themselves as a little child. (See Matthew 18:4.)

The mature Christian and church who walk this way of a little child are beautiful to behold and invigorating to be around.

Chapter 15

~

Kids Need Approval

EN WAS FIVE, but he was enormous. He took the beginner's class for basketball, baseball, and soccer, but it was apparent his sport would be sumo wrestling. He was at least three times as big and weighed thrice as much as the four and five year olds that were in any of the classes. When we played group games, he would use his weight to gain advantage and we would have to instruct him to be careful with the rest of the kids. We were constantly monitoring his play in order to preserve the lives of the other children. The reality was that if he fell on one of them, if the child lived through it, his or her body shape could be changed forever.

Funny thing was, though Ben was big, he was also fast. In the high five drill at the beginning of class, he kept up with most of the kids. And if they bumped into him while reaching to slap my hand, they would bounce off of Ben as golf balls do off of cement.

But Ben wasn't just big and fast. He was vivacious. He had more energy and a more outgoing personality than most of the kids in the program. And nothing seemed to faze Ben. If we corrected him or held him back from doing something because he might hurt one of the kids, he seemed unaffected. He never cried, pouted, whined, or sulked. He was just filled with size, energy, personality, and smiles.

That is why it seemed so out of character one day when Ben responded to me the way he did in the soccer dribbling drill.

Dribbling in soccer consists of moving the ball down the field (or in our case the court since we were teaching the class in the gymnasium) by tapping it with the insides of the feet. To stop it we teach them to trap it by simply placing a foot on top of the ball.

I am sure you understand, with four and five year olds in the introductory sports classes at the YMCA, it is approval, approval, approval. Everyone knows—parents, teachers and coaches—kids need approval. The younger they are the more approval they need.

When we do the soccer dribbling drill on the gym's hardwood floor, it is a fiasco of failure with the little ones. Their feet are quite clumsy. The soccer balls are bouncy. The floor is like cement and the kids are absolutely unskilled, especially during the first few sessions of the seven-week class. The balls go everywhere. Yet, as the balls are scattering all over the gym, I am saying, "Good job, Sam. Nice stop, Travis. Excellent dribbling, Sheila. Good trap, Julie—awesome, great, exceptional, superb." It's not lies. With each approving word, I saw one tiny good action. But for every good task done, there are probably ten done poorly.

A lap consisted of dribbling a ball from one end of the gym to the other and back. On this day as the kids finished their last lap, I was deeply engaged in approving of the kids even though it seemed that all of their efforts to dribble their balls were futile. But in my flurry of compliments to several of them, I hadn't included Ben. I turned around and there was Ben standing, holding his ball, and looking up at me.

Ben said, "What about me, Coach Chris? Did I do good?"

"Sure you did, Ben," I said. He hadn't done very well at all, you understand. His ball had been all over the floor on that lap the same as it was with most of the other kids; though that wasn't the reason I hadn't spoken approving words to him.

Ben persisted, "Then why didn't you say, 'Good job, Ben'? You told everyone else good job, but you didn't tell me."

I lied, "I'm sorry, Ben. You did an excellent job. I just forgot to say your name."

The answer I gave him seemed to satisfy him, but that moment with Ben etched a memory on my heart I will never forget.

I have observed people for my whole ministry and this is my conclusion. Adults need approval just as much as kids. The critical method doesn't work with adults any more than it does with children, because from the day we are born until the day we die, we feel inadequate as a result of our sinful condition. When Adam and Eve failed, we fell right along with them. The communion we forfeited with God and the resulting approval deficit we feel has left us wanting—no, needing—to hear, "Well done."

Yes we need correction. And yes, if people constantly lie to us about the sinful and capability realities in our lives, it could be detrimental to us. And I'm not suggesting that adults need approval with no correction anymore than kids do. I'm saying, kids need approval and nothing changes when we become adults.

Any healthy parent with kids knows the approval rule: ten compliments for every correction.

When I substitute taught school for a year, one kindergarten teacher acquired my services for her class by using the call system for the school district in which I was working. She didn't know me, nor had she heard anything about me because I was new in the system that year. She threw her need into the system, and I happened to pick it up randomly.

This teacher was very protective of her class, as all caring teachers are. But the sub she relied on had quit teaching that year. The day I substituted, she happened to be in the next room doing conferences with parents. So, on the sly, she observed my teaching of her kids with me unaware. The next day, after she affirmed it with her kids, she called me directly and asked me if I would substitute all of her planned absences that year. She gave me eight dates.

I asked her why she wanted me back, and she gave me three reasons. First, the kids liked me. Second, she said I worked well with her kids. But most importantly she said that I had mastery of the approval rule. She told me, "Not only are you sensitive to the kids' need for approval, you're enthusiastic about it. You aren't just approving, the kids really believe you approve of them."

That incident alerted me to another truth about approval I hadn't thought of before. Approval isn't just a compliment for a task well done, or for a good deed performed. Approval is an environment of receptivity that pervades in one's heart for another. And it even goes beyond that, as it is in one's heart for all people whom that individual encounters. That is, the person finds ways to approve of anyone and everyone. Furthermore, it has to tap every circumstance, every moment, every life. Approval has to be about everything. We have to find ways to give approval in every aspect of people's lives because that is where people need it—everywhere! Approval needs to be about performance; about talent; about looks, personalities, tasks, heart, desires and wishes—to mention a few. Approval isn't just about what a person docs—it is about who a person is. And therein lays the crux of the matter. People need to know we approve of them.

When the disciples put off the parents who wanted Jesus to bless their children, they were showing a kind of disapproval of both kids and their parents. They had missed the whole point of the heart of ministry. Jesus' rebuke to the disciples shouted to them, "I approve of people; parents, kids, adults; their hearts, their desires, their lives. People receive my whole-hearted endorsement."

In this same kindergarten class, the last time I substituted, a little girl named Asia (not her real name) asked me a question. She said, "Mr. C. (what I had the kids call me—a long story so don't ask), my daddy is picking me up after school. Please don't leave until he gets here, I want him to meet you."

All day long Asia kept reminding me. When I sat at her reading table, when we went to lunch, when we had recess and at story time, all day she continued to remind me, "I really want my daddy to meet you, Mr. C., so please could you stay after school until he gets here?"

I wasn't sure why Asia wanted me to connect with her father, but I perceived it was important to her. So I assured her I wouldn't leave before I met her dad.

When the end of the day arrived, I stood with Asia outside as the other kids' parents retrieved their children.

Asia kept saying, "Mr. C., I know he is coming. He should be here any minute."

Finally, I had to bring Asia to the office—as was the custom at this particular school when parents are late picking up their kids at the end of the day. I could see the disappointment on her face, but I told her I would stay in the classroom so that when her father arrived she could bring him there to meet me. I told the secretaries in the office about it so they could help the situation along as well.

After about ten minutes, it dawned on me they hadn't come yet, so I went back to the office and found that Asia was gone. The secretaries said that her father came, but when she told him about meeting me he remarked that he didn't have time, so they left. Asia hung her head in disappointment as they walked out the door.

I didn't need to meet him, and he didn't need to meet me. But Asia needed for us to meet. What would it have taken—a minute, two? All the way back to the classroom, all the way home, and to this day I feel bad for Asia.

How often do we disapprove of children's wishes and in so doing we disapprove of them? And as I say this, I have to ask as I did earlier, "Is it any different for adults?"

It is my observation that churches and Christians are notorious for communicating disapproval. We don't know how to speak the truth to people without disapproving of them. We have a heart to help, so we correct them, guide them, and exhort them. But in the end they wind up feeling devalued.

Earlier I referred to what I call the "critical method." This is actually a term that is used in Bible interpretation. But I have adapted it for my own purposes. I use it to describe the posture of so many churches and Christians that feel they need to point out people's spiritual thinking errors, their misinformation, their shortcomings, and failings in order to help them gain a greater maturity in the

Lord. Their intention sounds noble but the problem is that most of those who embrace this method are unaware of the important rules I have addressed in this chapter.

One, people need approval in every aspect of their lives. Two, the approval rule is ten to one—approvals to corrections. Three, approval requires an environment of receptivity. Four, where Jesus is concerned, people receive His whole-hearted approval regardless of their shortfalls.

Early in my ministry people couldn't say they felt approved of by me. I had my opinions about how people should be and if they didn't meet up to my standards for them, I spoke up. If someone didn't agree with me doctrinally, I told them where they were wrong. If someone had a wrong answer, I corrected them. If someone made what I saw to be an unwise choice, I was quick to point out their error. If a person performed a task incorrectly, I promptly identified their deficiency. What I didn't realize was I was creating an environment where people were questioning my approval of *them*. That is an uncomfortable place for anyone to be.

Over the years I have discovered something about the critical method. While it can guide some people in correct directions—more often it will guide people away from the correction. Here is the reason why: it looks too much like disapproval of people. So in my latter—hopefully more maturing years—I have tried to be sensitive to ways God might teach me to genuinely approve of people. And as I do, I try to help them feel my approval, even though their tasks, deeds, doctrines, or behavior may be less than perfect.

Here are some of the things I have learned that help me create an environment of approval about me:

1. I know people are victims of dysfunctional upbringings in varying degrees. This creates great havoc, a lot of mental baggage, and a great deal of emotional issues in people's lives. This knowledge helps me to be more tolerant of people's actions than I would be without this awareness.

2. I know my own dysfunction may have bearing on any critical views I may have of them. All too often over the years, I have seen my own emotional baggage (low self-esteem, etc.) become entwined in my judgments of people. I say this to my shame. Yet, there is good news. I have learned to exercise more patience with people as a result.

3. I know humans are characterized by a myriad of failures. Cases in point—are my own failures. To point out other people's failures is to showcase my own.

4. I have learned about personality types, and I understand the differences, drawbacks, and strengths of each. Consequently, I am able to accept people the way God made them much more readily than I ever could before.

5. I know about spiritual gifts and the accompanying strengths and abilities of each—as well as the weaknesses of each. As a result, I find myself able to focus in on the potential of a person rather than their inabilities.

6. I know certain religious environments create religious attitudes in people that they may have genuine trouble sorting out or shedding.

7. I know there are many cultural issues and mindsets in our day that are very confusing to people and create a lot of function ability problems in people's lives—problems they don't even understand, let alone have the ability to sort out.

8. I know this fragmented culture we live in creates such great confusion in people's thinking concerning God, the church, and spiritual things that they don't have a clue as to how to negotiate their way through the varying opinions, let alone sort them out.

9. I know sinners are dead in trespasses and sins and haven't the slightest understanding of spiritual things. This helps me love and accept them in spite of their sinful condition. I also consider myself a sinner the same as they are—saved only by God's grace and from no merit of my own.

10. I know some people will never change. So I am best to love them as they are rather than risk them feeling my disapproval by trying to change them.

11. I know some Christians will be in heaven even though they don't agree with me on some things— and in the final analysis, that is all that matters.

12. I know teaching is a powerful method of communication if it is truthfully, timelessly, and lovingly presented. So why risk people feeling disapproved of by correcting them when instruction can be a more effective catalyst for change?

There are more, but I'm sure you get the idea. Put all of them together, and I am able to find approval in my heart for some pretty despicable characters.

Yet, the most important lessons I have learned about approval come from the life of Christ.

We all know Jesus picked a sordid group of uneducated and unsophisticated individuals to be His disciples. Yet, He saw in them what no one else could see. And He approved of them right from the start. His environment with them was approval. He called them His friends. (See John 15:15.) Jesus did correct them. Over and over again, after a failure, a misunderstanding, a spiritual confusion, or a foolish statement, He would sit them down and teach them or help them understand what they had done or said wrong. In fact, more than once, He spoke strong words to them. Like the time He said to Peter, "Get behind me, Satan" (Matt. 16:23). Only a strong environment of approval, for not only Peter, but for all the disciples, would allow an intense rebuke such as this and still cause the disciples to feel accepted by the Master.

Jesus' treatment of the disciples as they made huge mental and verbal blunders and His approval of the Gentiles,

Samaritans, tax collectors, and sinners all combine to demonstrate the aura of approval that billowed around Jesus wherever He went. It was a thing of beauty that wherever Jesus went, people flocked to His approval.

I'm sure you can see what I am getting at. Our churches and our Christians need to radiate an environment of approval; not correction, not judgementalism, not finger pointing, not brow beating, not eye rolling, not criticism, or the like.

People need approval and lots of it. They need believers to communicate their love and acceptance no matter what they have done, how they look, where they have come from, how they've been raised, or what they believe.

One of the beautiful aspects of Jesus' presence was that anyone—I mean anyone—could come into it and find approval. When lepers came to Him, though the Levitical law said you must not touch a leper, Jesus ignored the stipulation and touched the diseased people. Can you imagine the feelings of worthlessness they must have felt every time they heard the words, "Get away from me!" or "Don't touch me!" or "You're unclean!" Can you fathom how completely dejected they must have felt as day after day, week after week, month after month, year after year; no one would touch them, come near them, or value them in any way.

They were disapproved of by everyone, except Jesus. Yet, He confirmed His approval with His touch. (See Mark 1:40–41.)

When the Pharisees threw a woman they had caught in adultery at Jesus' feet, He didn't look to disqualify her. He found reason to approve of her, even though she was a blatant sinner, her sin even defying one of the top Ten Commandments. (See John 8:1–12.)

The woman at the well in Samaria also received Christ's approval. She was a heathen, a woman, and a sinner. She had been divorced five times and was living with someone else's husband at the time. Yet, Jesus not only talked to her about spiritual things, He also pursued her spiritually and used her as a springboard to convert and approve of many other Samaritans in her town. (See John 4:3–42.)

Jesus approved of Zacchaeus, a despised sinner and chief tax collector. (See Luke 19:1–9.) Jesus approved of Levi (Matthew), a hated sinner and tax man, even inviting him into His *dirty dozen* (Luke 5:27–32). Jesus approved of ardent sinners and spiritual rejects from Jewish society on a regular basis (Luke 15:1–2).

Jesus approved of sinners, diseased people, social outcasts, heathens, Gentiles, the demon-possessed, and every manner of individuals the social norms of His day dictated you were supposed to disapprove of. Did he condone their sin? No! Did he approve of them? A whopping yes!

What does that tell us about our churches and church members? Who should we be approving—that we are not? And who should we be disapproving—no longer?

I wonder how many proverbial ladies caught in adultery, women at the well, sinners at the tax office, crazy people possessed by demons, people beaten by robbers, or just plain hurting folks for whom Christ died have we let slip out of our grasp because we couldn't find a way in our hearts to approve of them? And how many people have we alienated because of their sin—or appearance—or reputation—or class—or race—or status in the community; and because everything in the environment of our hearts kept defaulting to a spirit of disapproval.

Oh God. Forgive us. Cleanse us. Fill us with Your Spirit and Your heart to find approval for people at every level of sinfulness and disgust. Don't allow us to think for a second, that our disapproval has any beauty in it whatsoever, or that it is pleasing to You.

Can you see the beauty of approval in Jesus? He is the head of the church and wants this beauty to be seen in His bride as well.

Chapter 16

~

Kids Let It Go

I KNOW A MAN, Kit, who has a brother that won't forgive him. No matter how hard he has tried to win back his brother's friendship, the brother has refused to budge. Phone calls, letters, emails, cards, pleading, praying— nothing has persuaded the unforgiving brother to let it go. Kit has even gone so far as to accept responsibility for the initial parting of their ways that took place nearly thirty years ago, though it is clearly not his to take. And still his brother refuses to let it go.

Judy's father won't let it go either. Judy said some- thing to her dad on a Thanksgiving many years ago, and he has never forgiven his daughter for the verbal mishap. It wasn't an especially harsh statement. Judy only meant in jest to remind her father of a promise he made to her. But it got under the father's skin so—and he has let it fester so—that now it is a twenty-year-long grudge. It has become so out of proportion in his mind, he has imagined an elaborate scheme of hatred in his daughter's heart for him—so evil and so wicked that in his mind he thinks she must be taking her cues from the Devil himself.

Angela hasn't talked to her mother in fifteen years. Her mother shamed her at a family gathering in the early nineties in front of a few friends Angela had invited, and the bitter daughter has been unable to let it go.

Darlene doesn't even know what she did to offend her brother. And he won't connect with her long enough to explain it to her. She has begged him by letter repeatedly to consider reconciling with her, but he won't even dignify her letters with a response. It seems he has actually set his heart against letting it go.

We adults think ourselves so smart when it comes to discerning the intents in people's minds and hearts. We think about what must have been going on in the minds of certain people when they said what they said—or did what they did—and we determine the debauchery in their intent. Then we act as attorney, judge, and jury; we execute the sentence, and often it is a lifetime of bitter rejection for the person found guilty. And more often than not, the sentenced person has held his or her own trial and found the accuser guilty in the same way.

We call it smart. But isn't it just a pride issue?

Whatever the cause, we felt hurt, shamed, put down, embarrassed, ripped off, taken advantage of, or overpowered. And because our pride has been pricked, we refuse to release it—holding on as a protective measure for our own self-assurance.

Sometimes we resort to even more sinister reasoning. We will look at our own carnal motivational capabilities, and then analyze the other person's intents based upon what we ourselves know we are capable of. Then from this we will determine the despicable intent that must have been in their hearts. And we conclude: how can we let it go considering the lowly motivation they must have stooped to? But it's all because we are capable of the same evil. And then we call it smart.

Sometimes we ourselves merely feel powerful as we hold onto a grudge. We feel in control and so we will hold onto the power as long as we can.

Sometimes we simply punish the person who hurt us by not giving in, not letting go, or not giving up. Even if it was just a slip of the tongue, a moment of carelessness, a simple misunderstanding, or a word spoken in jest, we want people to pay their whole lives for hurting us in a moment. We reason, "A lifetime of punishment for a moment of hurt...seems fair to me. They'll be sorry."

Adults hang onto things because of pride, in order to punish, to feel powerful, because we think we're smart.

But kids let things go.

Maybe it's because kids aren't world-wise. Maybe it's because they aren't interested in power, punishing anyone, or being smart. Maybe it's just because they forget.

One day when I was substituting for a kindergarten class, Freddie was being stingy at the listening lab. I was shorthanded so there were no extra adults to help with oversight. Freddie had already taken the best earphones from one of the girls in his group—by force. She was whimpering. There weren't enough books so he was supposed to share his with the student next to him, but he was refusing to do that. Freddie was also controlling the tape recorder that played the story while the kids followed in their books. I heard a faint chorus of, "Mr. C....Mr. C.," coming from that corner of the room. When I arrived, Freddie was in his own little self-absorbed world of egocentricity, looking deeply into his own book, his ears covered with earphones, his fingers on the recorder's buttons, and listening to whatever he darn-well pleased.

I pulled Freddie's earphones off of his head so he could hear me and scolded, "Freddie, what are you doing? Do you think you are the only one in your group?"

A little shocked and embarrassed because I surprised him, Freddie looked up at me with his eyebrows furled into a position that reflected the anger in his heart.

I continued scolding, "Freddie, you know you have to share at this lab because we don't have enough books for everyone. And why are you stopping the tape? All right Michele, you take control of the tape recorder. Freddie, you give your book to Sarah."

Freddie furled his eyebrows even deeper in disgust because I wasn't just scolding him and shaming him for his behavior in front of the other kids. I was taking his control away from him. If looks could kill, I would have fallen dead on the spot.

Freddie burrowed his head, face, and shoulders down into a corner and went into a full pout. He wasn't crying. He was mad.

To insure he didn't take back control, I appointed one of the other kids in the group as guard and reporter. "Derrick," I said, "You let me know if Freddie tries to take over again."

I had lost a friend in Freddie. It was all over his face, at least what I could see of it. It was buried down beneath the table refusing to come up for air, in an effort to let me know just how disgusted he was with me for not letting him do what he wanted.

Sensitive to having lost a friend, about five minutes later I came back over to the lab and tapped Freddie's still buried shoulders. He turned and looked at me but nothing had changed. His eyebrows were still wrinkled in anger, and he was now moving his lips and gritting his teeth in disdain.

I asked, "Are you going to be OK, Freddie?"

In response, he squinted his eyes and yanked his head back into his tiny corner of spite.

A few minutes later the groups changed positions. I looked up as the kids moved to their next stations. Freddie moved as well but he did so with jerky deliberate movements to show his disgust. He stood up angrily and shoved his chair back under the table he was sitting at in irritated fashion. He then twisted his body around and stomped over to his next learning table. His face was still distorted in anger. When he arrived at his chair he plopped down, folded his arms, and continued his pout-fest.

I forgot about it after that. The lab time was about fifteen minutes long, and I was seated at the reading table.

In ten minutes I heard a little voice behind me say, "Mr. C., do you like my drawing?"

I turned to see who it was, and there was Freddie. He had a smile on his face and was holding up his paper proudly for me to see.

I said, "That looks great, Freddie. I love the colors you chose."

And that was the end of it. Freddie and I were best buds again. It was as if nothing had ever happened, and it wasn't just for that day. I substituted two more times for that class again that year and his anger never resurfaced.

Because kids let things go.

In an earlier chapter, I talked about the beauty of an environment that provides for patterns of accomplishing reconciliation once unforgiveness has set in. That is beautiful but this is different.

Here I am saying how much more beautiful it is when hearts are able to let things go before any hint of bitterness even has a chance to take hold.

In one area where I was a pastor, there was a church that was led by a man who was very gifted. His church was quite large—about fifteen hundred. This pastor had also received some national acclaim.

Growing up, however, this man had not been fortunate enough to have had loving parents. He had been abandoned by both his mother and father and had spent large amounts of time in an orphanage. This created a great deal of anger in his heart which was never dealt with. When he was saved and called into the ministry, huge changes occurred—but the underlying anger issues never left.

When this pastor's church began to grow, he found himself working closely with a ministry team in a multi-staff situation. When the stresses and rigors of the ministry began to present themselves with increased regularity, this gifted leader wasn't able to rely on his charisma and personality to maintain order. He found himself boiling over in anger and mistreating his colleagues with increased regularity.

There were two reactions from his staff.

One reaction manifested itself with varying degrees of spite and bitterness. If they weren't fired, they quit with fire in their eyes. Most of these angry former staff members became embittered sheep without a shepherd. They quit going to church altogether and formed an unorganized coalition of former pastor-haters. Different groups of them would get together from time to time—the whole binding tie being: communication about how unkind their former pastor had been to them. Of course they never called it loathing, hating, or disdain. That would have been sinful.

I don't remember how I became connected with one of these persons, but I will never forget my meeting with the man. We met over lunch and by the time our simple meal was over, I felt so dirty and grimy from the mud and slime he had slung concerning his former pastor, I thought I should go home and take a shower. It was one of the ugliest encounters I had ever experienced. At one point I could have sworn I smelled the foulness of the enemy's breath as I listened to the man. At that meeting, he told me of the abusive treatment, and the twenty-some families of former staff and church members that were wandering about without a church—meeting and crucifying their former pastor regularly.

I also had occasions when I ran into a few of the other families he referred to, and my encounters with them were no better.

The other group of staff members under this pastor responded differently. They all knew their pastor had some problems, but were able to allow his careless remarks to roll off their backs as water does with ducks. They seemed to take to heart their pastor's attempts to deal with his personal demons—where the other group did not. When he admitted some of the pain he felt from his upbringing to his church in sermons, it created understanding in their hearts. When he shared with his staff that he was seeing a counselor to help him sort out some of his issues, it produced patience for him in them. When he indirectly asked for forgiveness through his confessions to the church, they granted it. All of it helped them to never let anger and bitterness take hold in their lives.

This second group of people made up those who were appointed to take over the church when the pastor resigned. This was the case largely because they were still around. The result was a church and staff characterized by an environment of sweetness and beauty instead of bitterness and ugliness.

The past few years I have noticed a significant change taking place in my heart. It isn't something I noticed and determined to change. It's not something I looked at and decided to adjust. It is something I simply became aware of about me.

It is this: nothing is as serious as it used to be. Not the failures or criticisms of others. Not the rules, issues, or regulations that people try to impose on others. When people fail, I know it's OK because everyone fails and they will learn from their failures. Concerning myself, when I am criticized I know it is fine because I am comfortable with who I am, who God made me, and what He has called me to do. I also know that if I ever do something incorrect that warrants criticism, I'm good with that too, because I am capable of error as well. And I know when people try to restrict me with their rules or opinions, often it is a result of their own personal issues that may go back as far as their upbringings. Their issues with me are probably not because of me. And even if they are because of me, I'm OK with that as well, because I am becoming increasingly comfortable with myself in my own skin.

To clarify, I'm not suggesting that I am completely together. Believe me, I am as insecure as the next person concerning my own self-concept. I am just saying that as

I mature as a believer in Christ, in increasing degrees, I am learning there are a lot more reasons to let things go, rather than hold onto them.

When Freddie let it go, something in his little heart or mind caused him to forget all about it, and it's because something more important came up. He wanted to play, connect with his friends, or engage in a new project, so the issue lost importance. Perhaps not as perceptively as an adult might, Freddie discerned that other things were simply more vital than the issue that arose at the listening lab that day. It wasn't that serious for Freddie anymore, because something more essential came up.

One of the flaws of our humanness is that we foolishly place importance on being right at the expense of a host of many more important things. In people's minds, as foolish as it sounds, some of us will hold onto being right about an insignificant issue, considering being right more important than our very lives. It is like the monkey that won't let go of the morsel of food in the jar because it sees it as a prize and will hold onto it at the inevitability of its own capture. And people hold onto being right with the same foolish intent as the monkey, at the inevitability of their own demise.

How many relationships have we squandered because our pride was pricked, and we felt it was more important to be right than vulnerable? How many families have been tainted by spite because one party took too seriously the jest of another? How many friendships have been cast aside because people thought the issue was more important than the relationship? How much ugliness has surfaced in life because people took to heart some insignificant comment, joke, or remark? How many churches have been poisoned with dissention, hatred, and divisiveness because people couldn't discern that it was more important to let it go than hold onto their poison.

I think when Jesus said children are like the kingdom of God, this was one of the reasons. (See Mark 10:14.) Kids instinctively, or perhaps merely in childishness, know what is important, so they let things go.

In nearly forty years of ministry, I have seen a great deal of heartache, division, alienation, and hatred in people's lives and in churches. It is severely troubling to me. But I am only one person. There are a great deal more troubling relationship issues worldwide than I could ever even imagine. And Jesus sees every bit. And I think it is safe to say that just about all of it is rooted in people's inability to discern what is important. Consequently, they won't let things go that should be let go, and if they were let go, great peace would follow.

As I turned to see Freddie behind me that day, when he voiced his words, and his face revealed an accepting heart, I felt instant peace. I was relieved and felt a significant sense of joy that there was nothing between us anymore—even though he was a student and I was his teacher.

It is the same in our Christian relationships. Uncomfortable conflicts will always arise. But mature Christians know what is important. That is why they let things go. Mature churches also know what is important. That's why they foster an environment in their gatherings where people just know to let things go.

The more beautiful portions and persons in Christ's church have gravitated to the childlike practice of being able to let things go.

Chapter 17

~

Kids Care

THERE IS A concept that is quite unusual in Christianity called *spiritual gifts*. This concept is unique among all religious persuasions because it identifies the special God-given abilities and differences in people, and gives credence to their performance for the good of the church and the glory of God. Furthermore, spiritual gifts tend to set apart even the differences in the personalities of people and apply worth to those differences: so that people can say in effect, "God made me a leader, an evangelist, a giver, or a servant. I am able to be fulfilled and excel in that role. God has applied unique value and purpose to my life in my spiritual gifting."

These abilities, though people may show hints of their presence within them before becoming Christians, only surface in people's lives at the time when God's Spirit takes up residence in their hearts at conversion. In effect, God's Spirit unleashes the spiritual gift in a person's life.

One of these gifts is mercy.

Actually, mercy itself is different among the spiritual gifts in that it falls into a category that is unique within the whole collection of spiritual gifts. Mercy is a spiritual gift that only some people have, but every Christian should show mercy, at least to a degree. Other spiritual gifts that fall into this category are giving, faith, service, wisdom, and discernment.

But I want to look specifically at mercy in this chapter.

I know a Christian lady who clearly does not have a spiritual gift of mercy—not at all. I know several people who do, but this lady does not. Her name is Dayle. I have always felt that if the mercy content in Dayle's life were charted on a continuum—one being the lowest and ten being the highest—she would register at about minus three. Now, Dayle recognized this about herself and was fine with it. She would say confidently, "I guess I don't have a spiritual gift of mercy. God didn't make me that way."

One day I explained to Dayle, "Just because one doesn't have a spiritual gift of mercy does not mean Jesus exempts that person from needing to have mercy." I explained, "If Romans 8:29 tells us we were all predestined to be conformed to the image of Christ, doesn't it stand to reason we should all have at least a degree of mercy...that we should fall on the continuum somewhere."

She was a little disappointed. She enjoyed being her merciless self. But she got my point.

Adults, just by reason of their physical and emotional ability, naturally become polarized into personality, ability, and gender types. That is, if we are introverted as children, as adults we become more introverted—as a rule. If we are gifted in music and we discover that ability in ourselves, as we become older, we will find ourselves becoming more and more enamored with music. If we are leaders as children, we become even more that way as adults. And if we are servants as kids, as we move into adulthood, we will find ourselves becoming even more inclined to serve.

But when we are kids, the distinctions aren't so obvious. An example of this is that kids in first grade with artistic talent may give no hint of their future abilities. The strange stick figures on their parents' refrigerators will attest to this. And musicians may not show any outstanding gifting at this age. But one day I experienced something that alerted me to a quality in kids I had never seen before. I saw universal compassion.

While I worked at the YMCA, one of my titles was Sports Official. In this position I refereed or umpired baseball, soccer, and basketball games. I did this for kids of all ages, so I was able to witness the behaviors of children at almost every level. Basketball kept me the busiest.

You may be aware that the passion and element of competitiveness seems to increase commensurate with the increasing age level of kids. Children in kindergarten are much less aware of the need to win than kids in the fifth grade. And along with the increase in competitiveness is an accompanying, but decreasing, degree of mercy for the loser. By the time a kid is in the fifth grade (especially boys), he has learned to not just win, but, if possible, obliterate his opponent; while kindergarteners tend to just have fun playing and being watched and encouraged by their parents.

Coaches, of course, are always adults at every level. And coaches are assigned the task of teaching their team members to do their best, develop their kids' skills, and—almost in sinister fashion—manipulate a win. It is not this way with every coach, but it is with most.

In basketball, coaches teach their players how to play defense, shoot the ball, steal it from their opponent, and, in short, how to win. Whether the kids at a young age are aware of this or not, that is the overall objective of almost every adult coach.

On this particular day while refereeing, I experienced something that restored my faith in humanity as it revealed itself in the hearts of little children. I was refereeing a basketball game between two teams of second grade boys. The skill level of second graders is quite low, but the competitive spirit level is beginning to increase. And along with the rise of competition in the hearts of the kids, is aggressiveness in the coaches to encourage their players to do their best and win.

The coach for one of these teams was competitive at heart and knew basketball fairly well. I had seen his team in action before and knew he taught his kids, as effectively as one could teach second graders, how to play the game. And one of the fundamentals he taught his team was how to steal the ball from their opponent.

On this particular day in this particular game, one of the players on the opposing team was named Russell. Russell didn't play as much as some of the other second graders on his team because his parents didn't bring him to every game. Nor was he as skilled as some of the other players on his team. He didn't have any mental challenges; he just wasn't the jock type. You could tell his coach knew enough to make sure Russell didn't get the ball very much because every time he did, he would start dribbling fast and furious with his head down looking intently at the ball to ensure he dribbled it the best he could. That is dangerous because it is easy for an opposing player to steal the ball. And Russell would become so enthralled with dribbling and doing it flawlessly, he would seem to forget he was playing with other players, or that he was even in a game.

On this day for some unknown reason, one kid passed the ball to Russell in the back court. That would mean Russell could possibly dribble the ball all the way from one end of the court to the other. I could tell it wasn't in the coach's game plan for that to happen, because I was near the coach when he said quietly to the player who gave Russell the ball, "Sammy, I told you not to let Russell bring the ball down."

As soon as the opposing coach saw that Russell was in the game, had gotten his hands on the ball, and was dribbling with his head down, he started instructing his team to steal the ball. Russell was in a dribbling zone oblivious to anything else that was going on. It was a perfect opportunity for basketball theft.

The stands were packed as they usually were for this age group. Parents were yelling for their kids to steal the ball from Russell. The coach was yelling for his team to steal the ball from Russell. The extra players on the bench for the opposing team were screaming and responding to their coach's instruction—for their teammates on the floor to run over and steal the ball from Russell. But the five kids on the floor from the opposing team were frozen—frozen by mercy.

Each of them was looking at their coach as if to say, "We can't steal the ball from Russell. It wouldn't be right."

All this time Russell just kept dribbling with his head down, around the players, in circles, but nowhere in the direction of the basket. How could he have any idea where the basket was? He never came up—even for air. He just kept looking down at the ball that he was dribbling. And it was apparent that he was so engrossed in this task, he was oblivious to what anyone was saying because he never looked up or stopped dribbling.

Finally, every kid on the floor—the four on Russell's team and the five on the opposing team—started cheering for Russell. They were saying, "Good job, Russell. Keep dribbling. You're doing great." It wasn't long before the nine compassionate kids on the floor had led the entire gym filled with people, coaches included, to start cheering Russell as he dribbled. It was a sight to behold.

It reminded me of the words in Isaiah 11:6, "A little child shall lead them."

Eventually Russell came to himself, caught the ball, stood up, looked around, passed it to a teammate; and the game went on. But that thirty-second lesson from nine kids resisting the competitive juices within them—and the mercilessness of winning—stamped an indelible impression on my mind.

Kids care.

In Exodus 33:19, when God was preparing to show His glory to Moses, He made this statement. "I will be gracious to whom I will be gracious, and I will have compassion on whom I will have compassion."

It sounds as if God is stating His prerogative of preference, as if He were suggesting that because He is God, He can arbitrarily choose to show mercy to some and not to others, even if His mercy falls outside of His holiness. But if that is true, it is only part of what the scripture means.

God is also saying in this text (my paraphrase): "I exercise my right to be the merciful God I am; whether anyone likes it or not; whether anyone understands it or not; whether anyone agrees with it or not. I, as God, am entitled to be the gracious, compassionate, and merciful God I am."

Please forgive my liberties with paraphrase. But that is at least part of what God was saying to the historical leader of the Israelites. God has very clear and redemptive reasons for showing mercy to some, who in our minds may not deserve anything of the kind. God will not be pigeon-holed into our limited understanding of how mercy should be administered.

God is a merciful God. If we are like Him, we too are merciful.

But over the years too many issues confuse us:

Our personalities confuse us. Some of us just don't naturally gravitate to a heart of mercy. What mercy some may exhibit, we may not feel. So we assume we aren't the merciful type. We look at the "justice against injustice" attitude we see emerging in our hearts as being the way things should be, and we point our fingers at the compassionate ones, thinking them fools. But it is learned behavior. We have forgotten or covered up the twinge of compassion that was in our hearts during childhood. It gave way to the emergence of stronger personality characteristics. The mercy is still within us, but we have forgotten how to express it.

Our pride confuses us. We have been walked on or overpowered too many times, and our pride screams, "Don't be compassionate. It will come back to bite you. Someone will take advantage of you again just as they did a dozen times before. So hold back the mercy you are feeling. It isn't a smart emotion to express right now."

Our upbringing confuses us. We might think, "Dad wasn't compassionate. He was a hard-driving, eye for an eye, tooth for a tooth kind of guy. No one ever took advantage of Dad. Sure, he wasn't very tender to me growing up. He didn't give me many breaks. But it always worked for *him*. He protected our family and never let anyone take advantage of us. Besides, I'm not sure how one should show mercy since I never saw it expressed growing up. No, mercy is not something I should show or even know how to show to others."

Our own pain confuses us. We are so overwhelmed with the pain in our own life and family, we have subconsciously shut off our compassion sensors. If someone we see is in pain, we look the other way, not because we don't care, but because we can't deal with any more suffering.

Our self-centeredness confuses us. We are all inclined to think about ourselves anyway, and even more so as we become adults. But then we receive encouragement from the slogans of our day. "You've got to take care of number one." "If you don't take care of yourself, who will?" "God helps those who help themselves." We find ourselves philosophically agreeing with the Levite and priest in the story of the good Samaritan. (See Luke 10:25–37.)

Our perception of God confuses us. We might think, "I have asked God time and time again to have mercy on the people in my life who are experiencing pain. But He never seems to respond. Their pain gets worse and I feel as if He doesn't really care. Maybe it's because His mercy is not as I perceive mercy to be. Maybe it is because the Bible isn't accurate as it describes the mercy of our God. Or, maybe He has chosen not to have mercy on these people who are close to me. Maybe He doesn't like me. So I don't understand how mercy works at all because I don't understand how it works with God."

The result of the confusion is this: The twinge of mercy that has been in our hearts since childhood becomes buried under a pile of debris laden with misconceptions, misunderstandings, dysfunctions, and wrong information.

So, as adults, we lose our grip on compassion. We look at the hurting people around us and we turn our heads, we try not to see, or we stick our chests out proudly and choose not to see. Or we just choose not to care.

It's amazing to me how universal the lack of compassion really is. We live in a world that doesn't care.

Yet, by God's design, Christianity is intended to bring the gentle kid-like-ness in all of us back out of hiding—revealing once again the tenderness, the humility, the innocence, the compassion. When someone hardened by sin, granitized by the cares of this world, and crystallized by the confusion of life without God turns his or her heart over to the master, God resurrects the childlike qualities in that person. All of the tenderness and sweetness that was once in their hearts as children can come back again.

And along with it, God brings back the compassion.

I've seen it over and over again. People who were once hard-hearted, cruel, uncompassionate, and mean without Christ in their lives, became sweet, open, merciful, and kind once they became Christians. It is a miracle of conversion—yes. But I think the miracle can also be defined as a resurrection of the tender side of the child in people.

I have found over the years that the more I grow in Christ, the more I grow in my ability to discern the needs of people. I see the needs more readily, and I hurt for the people more completely. To be honest, there are plenty of things that get by me. But, just the same—I am detecting more these days. And if I have observed correctly, it is the same with anyone who is truly growing in the Lord.

Jesus made a pretty strong suggestion that this is the way it should be with His genuine followers. His authentic disciples should be compassionate disciples. (See Matthew 25:34–40.)

This passage in Matthew is really quite a scripture. It makes very clear the Lord's heart. One of the beautiful aspects of His church and His followers is that they are filled with compassion for the needs around them. They don't feed, clothe, water, or mend the less fortunate in order to win God's favor. They do it because the mercy in God has spilled over into them from them being in constant relationship with Him who is compassion, graciousness, and mercy. And then it flows out of them just as miraculously. They feed, clothe, water, and mend because they have become like God—again.

Chapter 18

~

Kids *Are* Innocent

O NE DAY I arrived as a substitute for a kindergarten class to find the teacher had not had time to prepare very adequate lesson plans for the day. She had left several books to read as fill-ins throughout the day, but the rest of her plans were pretty uncertain. So I was able to test my ability to fake it. And that I did.

I had arrived early enough to put some things together and look through the books. One seemed a bit peculiar for a coed kindergarten class, but I figured it would be fine for one day. Certainly I could make it work with all of my experience up to that point. So I put my time into preparing other things for the day. But preparation time goes quickly for a substitute when he or she arrives and nothing is prepared. I wasn't panicking. But I did rely heavily on the books she left, figuring it was the most certain plan I had, and putting the bulk of my attention into what wasn't prepared.

The kids arrived before I knew it and time flew quickly into story time. I had the twenty-five or so five year olds sit down on the floor in a tight circle in front of me. I pulled out the books, and I started with the one I had thought was unusual for the class, Cinderella. As I read the first page of the story, I thought it sounded a bit girlish, but I wasn't prepared for what I saw when I took my head out of the book.

Every boy in the class was doing twists, laying on the floor, burying their heads in their laps, protecting their ears, hiding their eyes, covering their mouths, plugging their noses, and yucking up their faces into contorted expressions—doing anything they could to keep themselves from seeing, hearing, touching, tasting, or even smelling the story. It was so funny I almost exploded in laughter. Instead I lightly scolded the male representation of the class and went on.

In less than a page I looked up again and they were all the way back into their "hear no evil, see no evil, speak no evil" postures. But this time, they were starting to whine, groan, and utter squeals of disapproval.

I shut the book and said, "I'll bet we can find another story to read."

The boys cheered. The girls fussed a little, but their discontent was a far cry less than the boys while I was reading the book. I chose the route of the lesser fuss.

Oh, the innocence of little children.

The dictionary defines innocence as, "lacking worldly knowledge or naïve, not tainted with sin, evil, or moral wrong, not maliciously intended, a simple unsuspecting person."

When I was seven, doctors told my father if he didn't move to a more arid climate, he was going to die. My dad had struggled for some time with an acute case of emphysema from years of smoking. He had been warned by his doctors before, but this time he took it to heart. So Mom, Dad, and

I pulled up stakes and moved from our home in western New York to Tucson, Arizona, in the fall of 1958.

Upon arriving, we found accommodations in a tiny, rectangular-shaped cottage until we could locate more permanent housing.

One evening, because I was bored and was yearning to make some friends, I wandered to a school a few blocks from where we lived hoping to find someone my age to hang out with. As I came around the back of the school, I noticed a large group of boys, some my age and some older, who were gathered in the playground in a group. It seemed as though they were trying to organize a football game. So I wandered in their direction hoping they would need another participant and invite me to play.

Sure enough, one of the older boys stepped out of the pack and shouted over to me, "Hey kid. We need another guy. You wanna play?"

I shrugged my shoulders and said, "Sure," trying not to reveal too much excitement at being included.

I was a little less enthusiastic, however, when I found out it was going to be a game of tackle football—no helmets, no pads, no mercy. A few of the kids were my age or a little older, but most looked to be twelve to fourteen. One must have been older, as he was old enough to drive the motorcycle parked nearby. I was only seven, but I was smart enough to know my ability to block and tackle a sixteen year old was, at best, minimal.

The game went on for some time. The owner of the motorcycle, also our team's quarterback, graciously sent me out for a few passes. I don't remember if I caught any, which probably means I didn't. When on defense, I managed to include myself in on a few tackles. But I was largely ineffective.

It was getting dark and there was talk of quitting. Our team had the football and was backed up against our opponent's goal line, which was marked by shirts and jackets of participating players. It was fourth down, so with dusk looming, and our team ahead by a touchdown, we all concluded it would be wise to punt. Our kicker lofted the ball far and high off of his foot, and the entirety of both squads swarmed to where the ball would drop, except me. It was my job to defend the goal line should the punt return man break out of the crowd, which no one expected would happen.

"We need a man to stay back," they said. But I'm sure it was their intention to keep me out of the way.

As I watched the pushing and blocking activity thirty to forty yards away, my eyes opened wide as the punt return man, with football in arm, burst forth from the pack. With all of his pursuit having fallen or become entangled with other players, he ran alone and full bore in my direction. He was one of the bigger kids, perhaps fourteen years old.

As he approached me, he looked straight into my eyes. I could detect a smile on his face that seemed to say, "This touchdown is going to be a piece of cake." I swallowed hard.

As he neared me, he darted to the side and I leaped at him with both hands grabbing for whatever I could get a hold of. I think my eyes were actually closed in terror as I jumped. But they found his two shoulders and gripped his shirt. His legs, pumping for all they were worth, continued in the direction of the goal line. But apparently my added weight onto his shoulders created too much of a drag on his forward progress. His legs ran out from under him, and he plopped to the earth onto his back. As he fell, I detected what appeared to be a grandstand full of cheers and shouts from the players on my team for the miraculous thwarting of a touchdown that had taken place.

Indeed it was a picturesque tackle to save the day. But somehow as he was falling, my body became turned around so that I was belly-down beneath him. He landed full force on the bottom half of my leg. The full brunt of his weight found my heel and flattened the front of my ankle to the ground. I screamed in pain and began to cry as a typical seven year would. Soon all the players were gathered around me. Not wanting them to think me the baby I was, I managed to pull back my wails to a controlled sob as they stood around me.

Wanting to comfort me, they said, "Wow, what a tackle. This kid's got guts. You saved a touchdown. I want him on my team next time."

I was in pain, but I was also enjoying the praise. I guess in a twisted sort of way, I was glad I had been hurt. It was a price to pay, but everyone knew who I was after that tackle.

The game ended with that. It was too dark to keep playing anyway.

Our quarterback said to me, "Hey kid, where do you live? I'll give you a ride home on my motorcycle."

That was the icing on the cake. From the back of his cycle, I directed him to our little cottage. He roared up our dirt driveway and my parents rushed curiously to the front door to discern the source of the commotion. I hobbled off the motorbike, up the steps, and through the front door which my mom was by then holding open for me.

My open-air chauffeur explained to my parents what had happened, while I laid down on the sofa in the front room. After a brief conversation with them, he started his bike and rumbled out of the driveway.

Tired from all the excitement, and yet with a certain amount of glee, I fell asleep right there on the sofa. When I woke up our cottage was quiet and dark—and I was alone. I remembered the injury to my ankle so I moved it slightly to test for pain. It still hurt, but not enough to keep me on the couch. I rose to my feet, limped to the front door, and then outside onto the small porch in the front of our tiny house.

The evening air was warm. By then darkness had fallen completely. The stars were shining brightly, and the moon was round and bold, but low in the night sky. I limped down the steps and around the side of our miniature home in an effort to gain a hint as to my parents' whereabouts.

As I stumbled around to the rear of our small home, I peered around the back corner of the building. As I did, I saw my father at the other end of the house sitting in a chair he had taken out of the kitchen. I could see his profile clearly in the warm Arizona night because he was positioned precisely between me and the bright glow of the moon. I wasn't sure where my mother was, perhaps shopping.

My father was leaning on the rear two legs of the chair back up against the house. He was unaware that I was watching, and for some reason I was content to keep it that way. As I observed in silence, he brought his right hand to his mouth. A small but distinct reddish glow appeared and brightened as he breathed in, which revealed the content of his hand. He then leaned his head back and exhaled. My eyes zeroed in on the sight and widened as he blew a cloud of smoke into the air—which I could see billowing in the glow of the moon.

Quickly but quietly, I stepped back from the corner of the house to ponder what I had just seen. I then turned and limped back around the front of our house, up the stairs, and through the front door. I lay back down on the couch again, but this time I cried myself to sleep. Why? It was simple. I thought my father, by continuing to smoke, was choosing to die and therefore leave me. To me, it was a clear indication that he didn't love me. At that moment all the joy I experienced earlier that evening was forgotten. The pain in my heart caused me to lose all awareness of the pain in my ankle.

But how could a seven year old understand the implications of addiction to nicotine? I obviously could not. I know now that this incident was saying nothing about whether or not my father loved me. He was simply enslaved to his habit. Then, however, in my innocence, I couldn't distinguish between hatred and habit—between anger and addiction.

Actually, my father later quit smoking and even drew closer to the Lord. And yet that one scene caused me to form coldness in my heart toward my dad which stayed with me until he died of emphysema when I was fifteen. Did he deserve that from me? No. But that is the way my mind processed the information it received that fateful day of emotional ups and downs. My innocence was interrupted that day by what my mind interpreted to be a shocking realization, and it adversely affected all of my perceptions about my father.

These days parents and most adults go to great lengths to protect a child's innocence. We send them off to bed or instruct them to leave the room when a discussion is brewing that might injure their innocence. We keep them from certain television shows and ban them from movies in an effort to not stain their tender consciences. We keep them away from Uncle Harry or Aunt Suzie because they have a way of corrupting everything they touch. We shelter them from child destroyers of every form because we don't want anything to disturb the natural process of their innocence.

Jesus took on the role of protector over the little children Himself. He said, "Whoever causes one of these little ones who believe in Me to sin, it would be better for him if a millstone were hung around his neck, and he were drowned in the depth of the sea" (Matt. 18:6).

Society for the most part knows instinctively, if a child's innocence is prematurely corrupted, there is a chance that this particular child will pay a price emotionally, mentally, and psychologically for the rest of their lives. And so we protect a child's innocence.

Even murderers in prison will get in on this role of protecting the children. If a child abuser or child killer is sent off to prison, it isn't uncommon to find that person dead under a table somewhere from a stab wound or head blow— because even murderers have standards. The innocence of children is something to be protected.

Yet we are learning today that protecting the innocence of children is becoming a daunting task. What with the divorce rate, the ever-declining moral standards on television and in music, the internet, an economy that requires both parents to work, and on and on; the period of innocence in a child's life is fast becoming a narrower and narrower window of time. Furthermore, it is becoming harder and harder to protect because there are too many influences bent on robbing our children of their innocence. Our children's time of innocence is shorter and their degree of innocence lesser than it has ever been before.

Before the fall and while they were still in the Garden of Eden, Adam and Eve experienced the greatest sense of innocence that has ever existed for a human on the planet.

They had never seen, heard, known, or experienced any kind of evil. Their minds and hearts were clean and clear of any hint of wickedness. There was no sorrow, no despair, no hatred, no frustration, no guilt, and no fear. It was much better than it is with children, because even a child is a sinner and can feel bad, angry, hateful, or ashamed. Adam and Eve had no idea what any of that was or even felt like.

Furthermore, Adam and Eve were adult in their thinking. Their thought processes were fully mature, yet still they felt no guilt or shame. Their minds and hearts were clean and uncluttered with debris from sin and separation from God. I am not sure any of us could ever imagine how absolutely glorious this state of innocence must have been for the first couple.

They walked with God in the cool of the evening and felt no intimidation from His holiness or purity. Second only to the beauty of God Himself must have been the beauty of perfect innocence without the encumbrance of any kind of pride or guilt in their hearts.

The innocence of a child isn't perfect. Nor is the innocence of a person who is born of the Spirit. But it is the closest thing we have on earth to the innocence Adam and Eve felt before sin entered their hearts. It can't be explained in human terms—nor can it be understood by human minds. But when a person experiences born-again-ness, something of the innocence of a child—and of Adam and Eve before their sin—comes back to that person. It isn't a stretch to assume Jesus' reference to born again in John 3 includes a kind of restoration of innocence. We can surmise this because just about every person who has ever been born again by the Spirit of God testifies that they emerged from the experience with a kind of restored innocence. It isn't the kind of innocence that left them naïve about life or devoid of the knowledge they had gained in their lives thus far. But they felt clean, full of love, approved of by God, trusting of people again, untainted by guilt, and refreshingly happy.

An example of this may be seen in ladies who in their pre-Christ years had been very promiscuous. But when they turned their lives over to Christ, part of the blessing of feeling forgiven by Him—for many anyway—is an accompanying feeling of restored virginity—not physically of course, but spiritually. The scripture does say clearly that God will remove our sins from us "as far as the east is from the west" (Ps. 103:12), and "will not remember your sins" (Isa. 43:25). And it says, "If anyone is in Christ, he is a new creation; old things have passed away; behold all things have become new" (2 Cor. 5:17). So scripturally there is precedence for a kind of restored innocence for those who have found forgiveness in Christ.

Within three months of fully surrendering our lives to the Lord, at which time of course, we were born again, my wife and I sensed God calling us into the ministry. So we packed up our house and family and went off to Bible college. It was the winter semester, and I arrived just in time to be able to play on the school's basketball team.

The second day of practice, two of the guys on the team got into an altercation and started a fist fight right on the court. Now remember, this is a school that is supposed to be filled with Christians called by God to become ministers. Afterward I voiced my innocent and somewhat naïve opinion of the altercation to one of the other players on the team.

I said, "I don't see how someone can be a Christian and punch another Christian in anger."

My teammate gave me some kind of an explanation about our righteousness being in Christ and not in our own merit, and no one is perfect. But I was still in shock. Here is why. I was still moving and functioning in the newly restored innocence that came over my life when I was born again.

Some will tell you that as we mature in Christ, the innocence of our born-again experience subsides and we become more informed and, in effect, streetwise in our Christian experience. They say we gain knowledge and understanding in the faith and we grow up in Him, so that we lose our naiveté concerning our new faith, and we become mature adults in Christ.

I don't buy a bit of it.

My observation is this. The more truly mature we become in Christ, the more our experience with Him teaches us how to retain and embrace a quality of innocence that is pure in Christ and grown up in His love. It's not naiveté. It's not denial. It's not immaturity. It is simply living nearer to God's heart.

Read the following scripture carefully.

> Love suffers long and is kind; love does not envy; love does not parade itself, is not puffed up; does not behave rudely, does not seek its own, is not provoked, thinks no evil; does not rejoice in iniquity, but rejoices in the truth; bears all things, believes all things, hopes all things, endures all things.
> —1 Corinthians 13:4–7

The most mature people in Christ's kingdom aren't so because they know more, have experienced more, are more intelligent, have more years as a Christian under their belt, or have more Bible verses memorized. The most mature people in Christ are so because they love more.

Have you ever heard anything so naïve and innocent as verse 7? "[Love] bears all things, believes all things, hopes all things, endures all things." It actually sounds like a description of a child living in a fantasy world. And yet the person who does these things as God's Word describes is approaching true maturity in Christ.

I have heard and observed many mature Christians confess their faith in, trust in, belief in, and patience with people just seems to get greater and greater the closer they draw near to Christ. While it seems outside of Christ, worldly wisdom insists, it is smarter for people to trust and believe in humanity less and less. They say we should be cautious, suspecting, suspicious, and careful in all of our dealings with humans. And they call it maturity.

Let's bring this discussion back to Christ's church.

1. Individuals or gatherings of individuals who have lost their innocence—who have begun to look suspiciously at everyone and everything; who don't trust, believe, endure, or bear up anymore; who judge, point blame, criticize, and find fault—are not beautiful, not by any means. It is laborious and grievous to be around people and gatherings like that.

2. On the other hand, people who still maintain the innocence and humility of their born again experience and their early associations with Christ are a delight to be around and beautiful to behold.

Which of these two environments would you like to settle into and grow in as you travel along in your journey with Christ?

To Contact the Author

~

Touch One Ministries
utouchone@hotmail.com